EUROPA ⚔ MILITARIA
SPECIAL N°18

THE MEDIEVAL FIGHTING MAN:
Costume and Equipment
800 – 1500

Jens Hill and Jonas Freiberg

THE CROWOOD PRESS

First published in Germany as
Krieger: Waffen und Rüstungen im Mittelalter 800–1500
By VS-BOOKS, Postfach 20 05 40, 44635 Herne, Germany

This edition published in 2015 by
The Crowood Press Ltd
Ramsbury, Marlborough
Wiltshire SN8 2HR

www.crowood.com

British Library Cataloguing-in-Publication Data
A catalogue record for this book is available from the British Library.

ISBN 978 1 78500 009 6

Typeset by D & N Publishing, Baydon, Wiltshire

Printed and bound in India by Replika Press Pvt Ltd

Contents

Illustration credits

All pictures were taken by Carl Schulze and Torsten Verhülsdonk with exception of:

Page 3: Image from the *Maastrichter Book of Hours*, Stowe 17 f.244, British Library, London
Page 4: Picture by Jürgen Howaldt, of the picture stone Hammers I, today displayed in the Bunge open air museum, Gotland, Sweden
Page 10: Mounting of cutout from MS 10066–77 f. 133v, Koninklijke Bibliotheek van België, Brussels, Belgium
Page 15: *Stuttgarter Psalter*, Cod.bibl.fol.23 158v, Württembergian State Library, Stuttgart
Page 16: Image of the picture stone from Etelhem, now in the Fornsalen Museum Visby, Gotland, Sweden
Page 22: Saxons, Jutes and Angles crossing the sea towards England. Taken from *Miscellany of the Life of St Edmund*, Bury St Edmunds, England, MS M736 fol.7r, Pierpont Morgan Library New York, USA
Page 27 Bottom picture by Thorsten Piepenbrink
Page 28: Image from *Tractatus in Evangelium Johannis*, Tours BM MS 0291 f.039
Page 34: Image depicting the capture of Carthage taken from *Chroniques de France ou de St Denis*, Royal 16 G VI f.441, British Library, London
Page 40: Image from *The Westminster Psalter*, Royal 2 A XXII f.220r, British Library, London
Page 45 Bottom picture taken by Chavi-Dragon
Page 46: Mounting of cutouts taken from the Winchester Bible, MS M 619v, Pierpont Morgan Library, New York, USA
Page 56: Image of the battle of Roncevaux taken from *Chroniques de France ou de St Denis*, Royal 16 G VI f.178, British Library, London
Page 68: Image of the siege of Vezelay Abbey taken from *Chroniques de France ou de St Denis*, Royal 16 G VI f. 328v, British Library, London
Page 73: Bottom image, of a battle for a bridge over river Seine, taken from *Chroniques de France ou de St Denis*, Royal 20 C VII f.137v, British Library, London
Page 74: Image 'Bellum/War', taken from *Omne Bonum (Absolucio-Circumcisio)*, Royal 6 E VI f.183v, British Library, London
Page 80: Image of Hector slaying Patroculus taken from *Troy Book*, Royal 18 D II f.66v, British Library, London
Page 90: Image of Gideon's Battle taken from *Chronique de Baudouin d'Avennes*, Royal 18 E V f.54v, British Library, London

Preface

For the purposes of this book, a 'fighting man' is considered to be anyone who had the freedom and the legal right to bear arms, while a 'man-at-arms' is a later medieval armoured cavalryman, whether of knightly or lower social status.

In medieval times the individual often needed to defend his life, his family and his property. Mercenaries earned their living by hiring out their skills, while feudal noblemen regularly mustered their men-at-arms and their subordinate vassals and tenants to provide military service, even to the point of leading them on Crusades to the Holy Land and elsewhere. In the later medieval period the growing cities required their citizens to take up arms as militia in defence of the community during times of external threat.

The sources upon which we have drawn for the reconstructions illustrated in this book are many and various, since each usually provides only partial information. The archaeological evidence for medieval material culture may come from single burials or mass graves, from the sewers or wells of castles and cities, less often from known battlefields, and occasionally from chance finds scattered across the countryside. Fortunately, great numbers of later medieval weapons and pieces of armour survived in the armouries of towns and castles, and are now displayed in museums all over the world. This physical evidence may be compared with iconography, and for the earlier centuries we are fortunate in having the illustrated manuscripts that were created in monasteries. The artists who painted these 'illuminations' for ancient Biblical and other stories interpreted them in contemporary terms; rich in colour and detail, their work gives us precious information about the clothing and war gear of the artists' own times. Each chapter of this book begins with an historical image, to show that the reconstructed warrior, armed trader, knight, man-at-arms or soldier is closely based upon historical sources.

The choices of materials, colours and patterns for reconstructed clothing are as close as possible to 'the real thing', but inevitably these can only be a matter of interpretation. Much knowledge of the necessary craft skills has been lost over time, and some materials are impossible to source today in appropriate quality. In the case of the early periods especially, original clothing is preserved only in fragments, and the cut of these garments can only be an educated guess based on the available iconography. All of the people portrayed in this book represent as closely as practically possible the appearance of times long past, achieved by studying all available sources, comparing the surviving examples, and experimenting with different craft techniques. This is an ongoing process driven by new documentary or archaeological discoveries, so such reconstructions undergo constant changes. Nevertheless, we have attempted to achieve a level of accuracy that can satisfy critical review by scientific historians.

Acknowledgements

A project such as this would have been impossible without the help of the persons shown in the photographs, and for each subject countless hours of research and reconstruction work were necessary. The authors and publishers wish to record their sincere thanks to all those who were willing to share their knowledge, and to give their time to pose for the photo-shoots. They are, in alphabetical order:

Bryan Betts, Andreas Bichler, Ralf Ebelt, Jonas Freiberg, Jens Hill, Ingo Kammeier, Christoph Ludwicki, Matthias Richter, Oliver Schlegel and the Archaeological Service of the Harz region in Quedlinburg, Gregor Schlögl, Burkhardt Schröder, Olaf Werner and the company I.G. Wolf eV.

Another debt is owed to Die Förderer eV for allowing us to use a harness made by Walter Suckert from the stock of the Landshuter Hochzeit 1475; this was made possible by Karl Heinrich Deutman of the Adlerturm Museum in Dortmund, Germany.

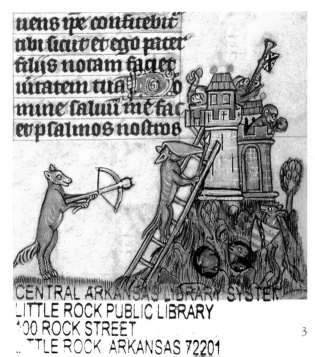

Viking Warrior

8th to 9th Century

Starting in the year AD793 with their raid on Lindisfarne, a monastery located on a small island off the coast of northern Britain, warriors from Scandinavia stepped into the glare of history: 'The harrying of the heathen miserably destroyed God's church in Lindisfarne by rapine and slaughter.' The Anglo-Saxon poet Alcuin lamented that 'Never before has such terror appeared in Britain as we have now suffered from a pagan race, nor was it thought possible that such an inroad from the sea could be made. Behold the Church of St Cuthbert, spattered with the blood of the priests of God, despoiled of all its ornaments.' These Norsemen gave a whole epoch the name we use today: the Viking age. The origin of the term 'Viking' is itself obscure: whether it derives from the Scandinavian word *vig* for a bay on the seacoast, or from the word *viking* to denote the activity of raiding, is still a matter of debate.

During the previous centuries Scandinavia had developed mostly in isolation from the rest of Europe. After the downfall of the Roman Empire in the West in the 5th century a large number of (eventually) Christian kingdoms evolved in the former Roman territories, all sharing a proto-feudal model of society. In some former Roman cities an urban, mercantile culture eventually not only revived but developed. Everywhere Christian monasteries became centres not only of religious life and learning but also, due to the craftsmen and travellers that they attracted, of economic power.

In the far north of Europe, however, where the Romans had never penetrated, the ancient pagan religion survived, as well as the old agrarian structure of society. The typical form of settlement was a pattern of small, mostly autonomous villages spread out over the areas that were practical for agriculture. Central institutions, such as the Church, and the secular kingdom with its feudal structure, were absent from these regions. Jurisdiction beyond the bounds of individual clans lay in the hands of the so-called *Thing*, a kind of people's parliament.

Due to the geography of Scandinavia, where mountains divided the farmable and therefore habitable territory into areas of modest size, and due to the consequent absence of central institutions able to organize the construction of interregional road networks, boats and ships became established as the main means of transport from prehistoric times. Unseen by the rest of Europe, a centuries-old tradition of ship-building eventually developed seagoing vessels able to cope with the harsh conditions of the North Sea and Atlantic. In parallel, the Norsemen developed navigational skills that enabled them to determine their position at sea beyond sight of land, making it possible for them to reach any point on the North Sea coastlines directly.

According to the latest research, a prolonged period of high birth rates in territories with only limited agricultural land caused overpopulation in Scandinavia in the late 8th century.

The consequence was that armed men set out in search of wealth, and, before long, of new lands for settlement. They sailed across the open sea in their long, narrow, shallow-draught ships, and rowed into bays and up river estuaries; the number of ships bringing men from the North grew year by year, and so did their radius of action. During the first years Viking raids concentrated on the coasts of the British Isles and Frisia, but before long they were attacking all round the shores of the Frankish empire. By the mid-9th century Viking armies had a permanent presence in Britain; soon large numbers of their longships were reaching cities such as Paris and Mainz, located far upstream on the great rivers of the European hinterland, as well as raiding the Mediterranean coasts of Spain and Italy.

The fighting man reconstructed in this chapter stands as a representative for those Norsemen, feared as warriors and admired as seamen throughout the whole of Europe. For a foreigner to encounter this completely equipped Viking warrior at the turn of the 8th and 9th centuries would have been an unlucky meeting.

His relative wealth is shown by the completeness of his gear. The classic round shield and the long spear, combined with a large knife, might be regarded as the 'basic kit' of a Viking warrior – the signs of a free, weapon-bearing man. For close-quarter fighting an axe (thought of today as the iconic weapon of the Vikings) might be carried; the long sword, slung in a scabbard at his left side, was a weapon reserved only for the wealthy, especially in the early phase of the Viking era. According to contemporary sources the amount of money needed to purchase such a weapon would have bought a medium-sized farmstead. Nevertheless, this precious object is outpriced by two other parts of his gear that immediately catch the eye. While the warrior of average means would have been protected by – at best – body armour made of several layers of cloth or leather, and a reinforced leather cap, this man is wearing a ring-mail shirt and a helmet made of iron.

The ring-mail shirt

Although the manufacture of mail armour in Europe predated Viking times by more than a thousand years, two main factors limited its use in 8th/9th-century Scandinavia. One was the simple cost of the material needed – more than 10kg (22lb) of good-quality iron. The other was the extremely time-consuming process of manufacture by skilled craftsmen, which made such protection very expensive. The raw material, normally traded in ingots, was first forged into thin rods, which then had to be drawn out into thinner wire during several successive steps of the process. In the next stage this wire had to be coiled around a metal-rod former into a spiral; dividing this spiral into segments by a lengthways cut along the former produced the single 'raw' open rings. These then had to be finished individually by flattening and overlapping each end, and punching holes through these to take the rivets that would be hammered in as the last step, after each ring had been interwoven with four others. More than 25,000 rings went into the manufacture of the mail shirt illustrated here; this *hringserkr* or *brynja* is made of a strong and flexible mesh, protecting the wearer's body against cutting blades and some impacts from thrusting points.

The length of this shirt is, according to the sources, typical for this early era. Longer shirts, reaching to the knee and below, equipped with long sleeves and worn in conjunction with mail mittens and stocking-like mail leg armour, are not found in the sources for this period. The only other use for mail was attached to the rim of the helmet, in a curtain to protect the wearer's neck and, sometimes, his lower face.

Since the ring-mail shirt only gives protection against cuts and, to a lesser extent, against thrusts, our warrior is wearing a padded jacket beneath it. Like the protective garments worn alone by less wealthy men, made from several layers of cloth or leather, this undergarment was meant to reduce the 'blunt trauma' produced by the sheer force of blows. Called in later centuries a *gambeson*, it was characterized by relatively soft padding (perhaps of horsehair, fleece or felt) sewn in between two layers of cloth.

The helmet

Like the ring-mail shirt, and for the same reasons, our warrior's helmet had a worth far beyond the simple cost of the iron needed to make it. The example illustrated is based upon a helmet unearthed from a grave in the Norwegian town of Gjermundbu, together with fragments of a mail shirt and other equipment. Finding remnants of only one of these items in a grave is quite remarkable; finding both on a single site may be called unique. The 'goggle-like' protection for the upper face is typical for one group of Scandinavian helmets, of which unmistakable fragments have been found in several other places. Earlier complete helmets of very similar types have been excavated from graves near the town of Vendel in Uppland, southern Sweden; these may date to as early as the mid-6th century, thus confirming a long Scandinavian design tradition.

The shield and weapons

The shield carried by our warrior, with a diameter of approximately 1m (40in) corresponds quite well to the preserved shields found in the late 9th-century Gokstad ship. That famous find included no fewer than sixty-four flat, circular shields made from limewood planks, with the outer edge bound with a sewn-on strip of rawhide; since the wood was only about 5mm (0.2in) thick, the shield was light enough to be manipulated easily in combat. The hemispherical iron boss in the centre covers a hole

Above: This portrait gives a good impression of the details of the Gjermundbu-type helmet with its attached mail curtain. In other contemporary societies the trimmed full beard and long hair might be a sign of high status, with only the wealthy having the spare time to devote to such indulgence, but contemporary sources tell us that when they had the leisure the Vikings took care over dressing their hair and bathing.

Opposite page: The weight and ballistic qualities of this spear make it improbable, though not impossible, that such weapons were thrown; they were for thrusting or cutting in face-to-face combat. Various sources show shields painted in halved or quartered patterns.

Left: The interior of the shield has a central bar grip, and also a shoulder strap for slinging it.

that accomodates the user's hand when he holds the shield by its bar-like grip across the centre of the interior. While the Gokstad shields were painted in either yellow and black directly on the wooden planks, this reconstruction is covered by a layer of cloth or leather, giving additional stability. The battle-scars on the boss and face show that this shield has already been carried into several skirmishes.

The spear, with an ash-wood shaft approximately 2.5m (8ft 2in) long, has a head of a leaf shape matching many finds in and beyond Scandinavia. Its broad blade makes it a general-purpose weapon, suitable both for hunting large game and, especially, for fighting unarmoured opponents, and its weight makes it practical for both thrusting and cutting. An experienced warrior could use this weapon single-handed, with the shield held in the other hand. Slimmer spears with narrower heads were used for throwing.

in central Europe the sword was not carried by an elaborate suspension formed from several laces, but simply looped onto a shoulder strap (baldric) fastened by a buckle in the front.

Clothing

Although we have already pointed out that the quality of his war gear identifies our Viking as a wealthy man, his basic clothing is mostly governed by practical needs – including those of somebody spending weeks at a time living on a small, usually undecked ship. His straight-cut tunic, reaching to the knee and with long sleeves, is made from a densely woven woollen fabric. This is not dyed, but is woven from yarn of two natural colours that allows the creation of a rectangular pattern during the weaving. However, the edges of the tunic are decorated with strips of patterned, tablet-woven braid made from dyed yarns. His trousers are closely fitting, made from wool with a felted surface that makes it to some degree wind- and water-repellent. On his feet are a pair of simple, undecorated leather 'turn-shoes'.

His leather belt is fastened with a decorated copper-alloy buckle and has a matching decorated strap-end, and supports at his back a slung pouch for small necessities. The contents of such pouches naturally varied. Besides such obviously useful items as a 'lighter' (consisting of an iron fire-striker, flint stone, and a supply of dry tinder), they might also contain a 'grooming set' (tweezers, nail-scraper, perhaps a small pair of scissors), a comb made from antler or bone, and even a sewing kit. Perhaps belying their popular image today, contemporary eyewitnesses reported that the Norsemen were vain about their appearance.

Above: The find-site of a sword would not reveal much about its origin, as warriors and traders travelled very widely, but comparing some details with the distribution of specific designs throughout Europe makes it possible to give a rough classification. This particular type of guard can be found in Denmark, the *Danelaw* (the settlement area of the Norsemen in northern and eastern England), and in the region of the Baltic Sea. The elaborate decoration is achieved by the inlaid 'damascene' technique, with strips of silver or copper alloy hammered into grooves filed in the steel. Sometimes the whole surface of the hilt was covered during this process, but most of the swords that have been found lack such decoration.

The sword in our reconstruction has a double-edged blade about 90cm (35in) long, and would have a shallow groove or 'fuller' down each side; this is a type quite common in the Viking era. The most desirable blades of all, often pattern-welded, were imported from the Frankish kingdoms, and would be fitted with more or less ornate hilts by Viking craftsmen. For the wealthy they were sometimes decorated with inlaid gold, silver, copper, or black niello, and fitted with metal, ivory, bone or horn grips. However, the swords carried by most everyday warriors were undecorated apart from the characteristic shape of the pommel, and were furnished in simple wood and leather. Scabbards were made of thin wood covered with leather, and often lined with waxed or oiled material or natural sheepskin to protect the steel against rust. Here the throat of the scabbard, its suspension loop, and the chape reinforcing its tip are made of bronze. Other than

Below: The bronze chape both decorates the tip of the sword scabbard and protects it from damage. The characteristic Scandinavian decorative style for this period showed stylized animal figures, real or mythological, interwoven in very complex patterns. Also visible here is the sewn-on tablet-woven braid, made from dyed woollen yarn, that decorates the hem of the tunic.

Above: The capture of prisoners for sale was one of the Vikings' greatest sources of income. Spain, which was under Arab rule at this period, was a major market for slaves, where customers were willing to pay high prices for sturdy European men and women.

Below: A skirmish outside the earth and timber ramparts of a major stronghold of the Viking period, perhaps in Russia. The tree trunks laid vertically on the face of the earth bank made it difficult for attackers to climb, under the spears and arrows of defenders on the battlements.

ulnerat a[...]

ud inuiat indomitos ferro sed claſſe furoreſ
t ſem uitiis pereuntib; omne receptu͛
uirtutiſ ſubpace cadit, trepida agmina meſto
anuertere oculoſ. ſtillabat uulneris index
errata de ueſte cruor. mox et pauor hoſte
ommunis adſtante͛ p dit. na palloz inore
onſciuſ audaciſ factidat ſigna reat'
t deprenſa tremejt languenſman & coloz AL
                                                bet'

Carolingian Landowner

Early 9th Century

In the year 800, King Carl I of the expanding Frankish kingdom (roughly, modern France, the Low Countries and western Germany) was crowned by the Pope as the 'Roman Emperor', thus renewing the claims of a unified Christian empire to authority over much of western Europe. During his reign Carl the Great – 'Charlemagne' – increased the territory of the Frankish empire to its greatest extent, but it was not to survive for long. By the Treaty of Verdun in 843 the Carolingian Empire was divided between his grandsons into three independent kingdoms owing nominal obedience to a single emperor; by the 870s it was descending into confusion, and in 887 it ceased to exist.

It was not only internal conflict that threatened Francia, however; the intruders from the North were pushing deep into Frankish territory, spreading ruin and terror. After their first seasons spent pillaging Frisia and other coastal regions, they began rowing up the major rivers deep into the heart of the Carolingian Empire. By way of the Seine, they plundered Paris in 845; they sailed up the Rhine and devastated Cologne in 862; and in 881 they reached the imperial city of Aachen, whose distance from a major river proved to be an illusory protection – the Norsemen often captured horses locally so that they could range further afield.

In the Frankish empire of the north-west European mainland the Vikings encountered a society in which the vigour of the 5th-century Germanic invaders had merged with the traditions of Roman antiquity. While the Norsemen still worshipped the old heathen gods, Carolingian society already had a 400-year-old Christian tradition. In the 9th century many of the old Roman urban centres had already regained their character. Although still much smaller than their predecessors, these towns consisted not only of new timber-built houses among the restored ruins of Roman buildings, but boasted several new stone buildings, of which the churches were the most impressive.

In this environment a society had developed with a distinct separation into different social classes. Beside the clerical world, whose monastic orders had not only preserved literacy but also made a significant contribution to the renewal of the economy, there existed a social system with a clearly defined rank and role for everyone, from the poorest farm labourer up to the emperor himself.

Right: The landowner is seen here with his full suite of arms. The heavy spear with its 'winged' head (note the sideways projections just beneath the blade) is of a type common throughout Europe, but the shield is completely different from that of his Scandinavian enemies. It is of convex shape, and has a protruding cone-shaped boss. Although archaeology has revealed no examples of this type, it is so often depicted in the widespread iconography of the period that we may be confident it is not just an artistic invention.

The Carolingian warrior reconstructed in this chapter may not be a member of the nobility, but, judging from his fairly elaborate clothing, he is clearly not a labourer either. He is a farming landowner, able to finance a higher-class lifestyle by trading in foodstuffs, livestock and timber from his holding. His legal status is that of a free man, and like his counterparts in Scandinavia he has the right to bear weapons; these are both a sign of his status, and a practical necessity of his duty to help defend his community. The sword is the symbol of this rank in society, and he would take it with him every time he left his farmstead.

This reconstruction differs from that of the Viking warrior in that it does not rely completely on the work of archaeologists. In the Frankish region the evidential situation is entirely different. Finds from settlements are quite rare, due to the repeated redevelopment of such sites that has taken place right up into our own day. One typical earlier source does not exist at all: grave goods. Christian tradition eliminated the former practice of burying the dead completely clothed and accompanied by their weapons and household items. The early medieval Christian was normally buried wrapped in a plain shroud, and it is rare (though not completely unknown) to find any surviving metallic objects in a grave.

Above: The two-edged *spatha* sword was worn on the left side from an outer sword belt; like the scabbard, this belt is handsomely decorated with copper-alloy fittings. The two-point attachment of the suspension straps keeps the sword from swinging about when the owner is moving. While the metal parts of such items have survived in some numbers, the leather parts must be reconstructed on the basis of period iconography.

Right: Another detail visible in these pictures is the cut of the tunic hem; unlike those of later times, this is notched at both sides to prevent any constriction when running or riding a horse. Note too the long metal strap-end decorations of the two belts hanging down the front; the braid decorated with discs applied down the front of the trousers, copied from several miniatures; the 'puttees'; and the simple shoes with a central seam up the vamp.

However, this source of knowledge is replaced by another: the painted illustrations in manuscripts. In this epoch monasteries produced manuscripts – not only Biblical texts or those dealing with other religious themes, but also transcriptions or translations of Classical literary works – and these were all decorated with colourful miniature paintings depicting aspects of the written content. The main purpose of these 'illuminations' was probably to convey the essentials of the texts at a time when a very high proportion of the population was illiterate. Although we must take into account that a good proportion of the detail in such pictures must have been governed both by technical limitations and by a degree of 'artistic freedom', they are still an important source for reconstructing contemporary costume.

War gear

The situation in which we meet our landowner is doubtless of a social rather than a military character. He wears elaborate, decorated clothing, and the absence of protective armour such as a mail shirt reduces his display of the spear and shield to a sign of his social status. If we did encounter him in full war gear, only minor details such as the convex shape of his shield and its distinctly cone-shaped boss would distinguish him from his opponent disembarking from a longship. Just like the Scandinavian raider, he would probably have worn a ring-mail shirt over a padded undergarment, and his head would certainly have been protected by an iron helmet. Again, no surviving example of an identifiable Carolingian helmet has yet been found, but the most common type was almost certainly a *spangenhelm* like that illustrated on page 24, with or without a 'nasal' bar at the front.

Earlier weapons associated with the Franks had by now more or less disappeared. A type of light throwing-axe called a *francisca* had once been common among the migrating European tribes; likewise, heavy single-edged swords had lost their prominence during the 8th century, although they seem to have survived for some time in Denmark. The most prominent weapons in the Carolingian armoury were pole-arms and two-edged swords; the latter was called a *spatha*, after the ancient Roman term for a long cavalry weapon. These would normally have been supplemented with a medium-sized knife, as suitable for use as an everyday tool as in its function as a back-up weapon.

Above: A not-so-common detail of the tunic is the V-shaped neck opening. This detail, together with that of the decorative braid added to the edges of the garment, is borrowed from a book illustration. The small cross-shaped *fibula* brooch is of a type popular over a long period.

Clothing

The costume of our country landowner, reconstructed on the basis of several period miniatures, corresponds with a style of Germanic origin that was common throughout most of Europe. Long-legged trousers of a close-fitting cut are gartered at the knee, below which they are covered with additional bandage-like lengths of cloth wound around the leg like 20th-century military 'puttees'. The long-sleeved woollen tunic reaches almost to the knee; beneath it a second, lighter tunic of linen was worn like a shirt (we must bear in mind that cotton was not yet generally available in northern Europe). This linen tunic was also suitable for wear as the sole garment in warm weather, and in colder seasons a cloak would be worn over both tunics (*see* page 14). The simple leather 'turn-shoes' are of a universal, pan-European type; no distinctive sort of Carolingian footwear is known. The ensemble is completed by a first, inner belt carrying a knife and a pouch, and perhaps a spare set of leg bindings.

Left: Our landowner is seen here in his full costume, including a cloak. From the drapery visible in a number of miniature paintings it has been possible to reconstruct this as of a semi-circular shape. It is tied closed at the neck by lengths of braid, obscured here; in this case the *fibula* is purely decorative.

Right: The glass beaker, from which our landowner is taking a welcome drink after perhaps returning from a journey, is of a type that originated in the Rhineland and the Ardennes but found its way even into the far North along the busy trade routes. The design of the decorative edging braid on the tunic is taken from a painting in the so-called 'Vivian Bible', today preserved in Paris. It is made from a linen band embroidered with woollen yarn.

Below: Battle scene from the 'Stuttgart Psalter' now held in the Württembergische Landesbibliothek in that city. Carolingian iconography shows many examples of soldiers wearing 'scale' body armour; this is so-called because of its resemblance to the scales of a snake, being constructed of many small overlapping iron plates, pointed or rounded at the lower end, sewn to a leather backing. Note also the helmets; they show the reinforcement and construction bands of the *spangenhelm* type, but appear to be 'tortoise'-shaped: two distinct side sections meet in a central comb, and the lower edges sweep upwards to meet over the brow. Like the Carolingian shield, this often-illustrated helmet type is so far unsupported by archaeological finds.

Scandinavian Trader

9th to 10th Century

Generally speaking, from the 6th century onwards the Scandinavians were the driving force behind the revitalization of regular long-distance trade, which had lain fallow since the downfall of the Western Roman Empire a hundred years earlier. The Norsemen's legendary skills of seamanship served not only their raids on the coastal regions of Europe, but also enabled them to undertake profitable long-distance trading voyages, by sea and river, across much of the known world.

The design of this trader's costume follows Asian traditions brought back from the voyages by Norsemen up the eastern rivers from the Baltic coasts deep into the heart of what would later become Russia – a country that took its name from these opportunistic raiders, merchant-adventurers and mercenaries. The 'Rus', the upper class descended from these explorers who came to rule the region around the River Dnieper, were probably responsible for spreading this fashion over the whole Baltic area, since they maintained a strong relationship with the home countries of their ancestors.

Clothing

The fanciest part of the trader's costume is the coat-like *kaftan*. Made from fine wool fabric and decorated with silk, it is a clear descendant of an Eastern tradition originating in ancient times. In the Baltic region this type of garment is quite well documented; men wearing them are depicted on 'picture stones', and the remnants of these garments are also found in graves. An important site is the former Swedish trading centre of Birka located on the Mälaer Sea, where several graves containing textile fragments have enabled archaeologists to reconstruct details such as the silk decoration. (These silk fragments are evidence of a trading network reaching as far as China.)

The graves also yielded silver fragments, indicating that these garments were even decorated with this precious metal. Another detail completely different from other contemporary clothing is the fact that this type of kaftan was closed at the front by buttons. Reinforcing this impression of wealth is the very baggy style of trousers worn by our trader; making such costly garments required three times as much material as the usual, more closely tailored trousers.

The coloration of both coat and trousers is quite bright even for today's tastes but, perhaps surprisingly, both these colours

can be obtained by using Viking-age dyestuffs and methods. The bright green of the kaftan is the result of a double dyeing process: as a first step the fabric must be dyed blue by using woad *(Isatis tinctoria)*, and in the second step it is coloured again with dyer's weed *(Reseda luteola)*, a plant used to dye fabric yellow since ancient times. As this process is quite laborious, and the resulting colours are not very stable – they fade fast in use – these colours are another sign of extravagance. The bright yellow of the trousers can be achieved by dyeing fabric in a decoction of fermented tansy *(Tanacetum vulgare)*.

Right: Taking his ease during a peaceful day at a trading settlement beside one of the great Russian rivers, our trader displays his wealth by his costume. As well as his silk-trimmed coat and the lavishly fabric-consuming cut of his baggy trousers, we can just see here his shirt, which is made not of everyday linen but of silk imported from the Orient. Even our traveller's cap is a relatively precious possession; it displays his superior means by its trimming of mink fur, and small silver decorations.

The Viking trader's world

Despite his elaborate costume and richly ornamented knife sheath, our trader would not have attracted any particular attention in the muddy streets leading up from the wharfs in one of the major trading centres such as Birka or Hedeby. These towns were visited not only by the population of the surrounding countryside, but also by traders and travellers from all the countries of Europe. The local authorities were keen to attract to their towns the exporters and importers of exotic, high-value trade goods. As well as raising funds by charging customs fees, they introduced special commercial laws to stimulate trade. One of these regulations allowed foreign traders not only to sell their goods during the dates of established market gatherings on a few occasions during the year, but gave them (or rather, sold them) permission to establish permanent commercial settlements that were allowed to do business all year round.

If we could imagine the sights, sounds and smells on a normal day in the markets of such a Baltic trading centre during the 9th or 10th century – crowded with merchants and customers drawn from all over the known world, in a noisy bustle of setting out stalls, displaying and inspecting the goods on offer, and multi-lingual haggling – it would conjure up a positively carnival atmosphere.

Below: The long, slim-bladed fighting knife is of a type that has been found on several sites all over the North. This close-up shows both the rich metal decoration of the sheath, and the combination of a straight and a Y-shaped suspension strap which ensures that the relatively heavy weapon does not swing about too much when the owner is walking. The undecorated pouch is made entirely of leather, including the toggle fastening of the flap.

Above: The metal belt fittings are reconstructed after a pattern found in the burial ground at Birka in Sweden. While the buckle is of simple steel, the riveted decorative plate and the strap-end are made from a copper alloy, embossed with a geometrical design. Note also, left of the strap-end, the dark brown trim down the front edge of the kaftan. This is made from a heavy silk fabric, and due to its cost only a fairly limited quantity is applied to the coat.

Below: The *armamentarium* of the trader, and the common currency of the Viking age. We see here a pair of brass scales, foldable for easy transport, with the associated set of standardized brass weights, and silver in many forms. The coins, minted in different European and Arab countries, are accompanied by silver ingots of full and half size, and 'hack-silver' – to make smaller pieces of currency for exchange, items of silver jewellery, ingots, coins and any other suitable objects were routinely cut into pieces. The complete ingot weighs *c*.130g (4.6oz), and was cast in a mould made of soapstone. This mould was found in a grave discovered in Norway, which also contained several different metalworking tools. While the European coins recovered by archaeologists were minted in different Carolingian kingdoms, in England, and in Scandinavia itself, the number of Arab coins found is relatively enormous. Rich silvermines enabled the Middle Eastern caliphate states, in particular, to mint plentiful coinage, which was used to purchase large quantities of Northern luxury goods such as furs, slaves, amber and honey. Ingots, complete items of jewellery and hack-silver are frequently found together with large numbers of coins.

Left: Helmets like this one correspond with a style that originated in the Slavic areas, and resemble, in their turn, other finds from much further east; they have been recovered everywhere from Poland to Mongolia. They are made from several separate plates riveted together and rising to a distinct 'spire' at the apex; this hollow tube was probably used to mount a horsetail crest, as illustrated. In contrast to most helmets found in the West, this type are often decorated, sometimes richly. Only a few original helmets are fitted with a nasal at the front, but most of them show signs of an attached mail curtain to protect the wearer's neck.

these took human form. While slavery itself was forbidden within the Carolingian kingdoms, the trade in slaves was not, providing the 'goods' were not Christians. Northern traders were active in this commerce not only in the North itself but also in Muslim Spain, using Carolingian trading centres as transition points. Violence was also involved in the acquistion of furs as tribute from Slavic peoples; cured pelts from the animals of the Eurasian heartland were in great demand in the Mediterranean world.

When he was in full armour – which we can certainly assume for a man of his means – our trader would have worn a knee-length mail shirt over a padded garment. His helmet may have been of the Gjermundbu or Valsgärde style or (influenced, like his costume, by Eastern contacts), of a 'spired' form similar to one

War gear

Although the costume of our trader is representative of what was worn while doing business or leading his normal everyday life, we should not forget that simultaneously he is also a warrior. Firstly, it is obvious that when on long journeys through almost unexplored country, carrying both currency and highly valuable goods, it was necessary for such travellers to be able to protect themselves and their possessions. Secondly, such merchant ventures were opportunistic, and military force was often an important means of acquiring trade goods, particularly when

Right: A 'table service' such as this would have been reserved for the wealthiest levels of society. The pitcher of black earthenware is of the type called 'Tatinger' or 'Frisian' ware, and is decorated with ornaments made from tinfoil. Like the footless glass beakers, its most probable origin was the Rhineland area, but vessels of both types have been found on sites all the way from the Frisian town of Dorestad to Birka in Sweden. They would have been seen in all important centres of trade, imported together with the wine that was drunk from them.

found at Giecz. But on the day we meet the trader he is dressed for a peaceful day at the market, and carries at his hip only a long, slim fighting knife in a metal-decorated sheath extending almost up to the pommel. Remains of similar weapons or parts of their typical decoration have been found in several locations all over the Baltic region; complete sets were found at the southern Swedish town of Valsgärde and in burial grounds at Birka.

Currency

As well as his knife our traveller also carries a belt-pouch containing not only the usual fire-striker, comb, etc., but also the most important tool of his trade: a foldable set of accurate scales and weights.

Above: Rare sets consisting of a number of small silver vessels have been found on only a few sites throughout Scandinavia. They are usually only a few centimetres across, but are made of heavy silver. Their intended purpose remains unclear; we may guess that they may have been used for consuming hard liquor, such as alcohol-rich fruit wines combined with herbs, spices or more powerful substances.

The main currency of the Viking age was silver. Central Europe and the Arab world had established monetary systems that relied on minted silver, with the worth of each coin guaranteed by a central authority. However, in Scandinavia and the Baltic region the means of exchange was by the simple weight of fine silver; the agreed price of an item was paid in silver in any form, compared against standardized weights. The core of this system was the 'mark', which was approximately 220g (7.75oz) of pure silver. According to written records, about 125g was the price paid for a sword, while a cow was worth 50g.

It did not matter whether the price was paid in coins, ingots, jewellery, or parts of these. This fact may have been the main reason for the popularity of massive bracelets made of silver. These not only displayed the wealth of the owner, and made it easy to carry it safely on his person, but could be 'hacked' for smaller purchases at need.

Left: Our trader has used a spear to stop a thief intent on stealing a precious silver vessel. A spear with a broad head to tear open big, heavily-bleeding wounds was as suitable for hunting big game as for battle. By contrast, this long, slim head identifies the trader's spear as solely a weapon of war, intended to pierce mail armour by a hard thrust to break a few adjacent rings. The two rows of eight small copper-alloy rods just visible protruding from the base of the socket are typical of a group of such weapons found only in Scandinavia. The 2.8m (9ft) ashwood shaft would make it useful for fighting either on foot in close formations, or from horseback.

Viking Warrior

Late 10th Century

While the warrior of the early Viking period portrayed on pages 5–9 started his raids in Scandinavia itself, the fighting man reconstructed in this chapter is representative of the greatest expansion of Scandinavian power in history. Living at the end of the 10th century, he too would call himself a Viking, but he might have been born in Iceland, Ireland, England, Normandy (which took its name from the Norsemen who settled there), on the continental shores of the Baltic Sea or the banks of one of the great Russian rivers. In all these far-flung regions Scandinavian warriors followed their initial raiding by settling down to found colonies. Some voyagers brought their families with them, but others married local women, thus producing merged communities within a few generations.

During the 9th–11th centuries Scandinavia also saw the development of centralized social structures. Kingdoms of different significance were established; their kings gradually converted to Christianity (although the old religion long retained its hold on the minds of the common people). In military affairs, at least, these sovereigns came to benefit from systems of national organization. While the rigid social hierarchy of the truly feudal countries (*see* pages 29–30) never took hold in the North, formerly autonomous areas did become, in the modern term, 'military districts', bound to the king and obliged to provide troops when he needed them. The exact numbers of fully manned ships that were to answer his summons were specified, and even the war gear that each man had to bring with him. This enabled Scandinavian monarchs to raise highly mobile and well equipped armies at short notice. The Danish kings, in particular, exploited these developments to expand their kingdom far beyond the borders of today's Denmark. At the end of the 10th century the Danish kings held sway over southern Sweden, Iceland, and – for many years – Norway; from 1016 to 1042 King Cnut and his heirs also ruled England.

Following the raids of the 790s, which had involved the crews of only perhaps two or three ships at a time, the Saxon kingdoms of England suffered some 200 years of warfare at the hands of the Norsemen. From the 850s onwards whole armies transported by fleets of hundreds of longships landed in England, campaigning in the summer and often staying over winter. Although King Alfred of Wessex and his descendants successfully defended the south and west, during the first half of the 10th century the whole north-east part of the country was Scandinavian territory. The Norse leaders extracted huge

sums not only in plunder, but in protection money –'Dane-geld' – in return for agreeing to restrain their warriors. According to contemporary chronicles, between the years 991 and 1018, 216,500 pounds weight of silver changed hands. (If we equate this amount of bullion with the contemporary Saxon currency, it would represent no fewer than 52 million silver coins.)

Right: We may imagine that this late 10th-century warrior is guarding the stockade of a temporary camp on the borders of the *Danelaw* – the region of Danish settlement in north-east England. In full armour, he rests upon his 'Danish axe', whose impressive dimensions can be appreciated.

War gear

Taking all this into account, let us assume that our warrior was born in the Viking kingdom of York in northern England. The quality of his equipment places him in the ranks of an army that is at least semi-permanently organized. Although ownership of a ring-mail shirt and a helmet was no longer a sign of extraordinary wealth, both were still valuable items. This limited their use to the nobleman and the 'professional' warrior, for whom they were the tools of his trade and his means of 'life insurance'.

During the past 200 years the ring-mail *brynja* had stayed more or less unchanged in appearance; hanging from the shoulders, it reached half way down the thighs and covered the upper arms. Longer shirts, covering the knee, are mentioned in some sagas, but did not become common until the 11th century. As before, a padded garment is worn beneath the mail shirt to protect against the bone-breaking force of blows.

The most impressive part of our warrior's gear is the long-shafted axe. While battleaxes played only a minor role in continental Europe, the Scandinavians had a fondness for this type of weapon. The battleaxes of the early Viking era still

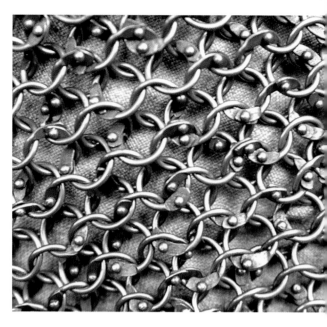

Above: Close-up of high-quality riveted ring-mail armour, which follows every movement of the wearer's body. Each of the rings, made of drawn iron wire, is conjoined with four others; mail with each ring joined to six others can be made, but is heavier and less flexible. A slightly cheaper type alternated rows of riveted rings with rows of solid rings. (Even simpler examples, with the ends of the cut rings simply overlapped and butted together, are normally of non-European origin.)

Right: Our warrior's sword-pommel is of one of the classic Norse 'lobed' designs. Note the heavy, riveted brass edge-guard on the knife sheath. The items hanging from the waist belt by a thong are a pair of tweezers and an ear-cleaning spatula.

bore much similarity to everyday tools, and some intermediate types were suitable for any purpose, from chopping wood to fighting. But the type of axe illustrated, which required both hands to wield it, was designed solely for war. With perhaps a 1.5m (5ft) shaft and a cutting edge up to 30cm (12in) long, it was termed a *breidox* ('broad axe'), or simply a 'Danish axe' – 'Dane' then being a generic Western term used of Norsemen, whatever their origin.

In the hands of a strong, skilled warrior this heavy weapon, whose force was increased by the swing of its long handle, could crush helmet and skull together, sheer through ring-mail to sever limbs, or fell a knight's horse at a blow. During the long wars in England between Danes and Anglo-Saxons, the latter may have copied this terribly effective weapon from their foes, or it may simply have been retained by the subsequently merged Danish-Saxon populations in the north and east. Either way, the elite Saxon *huscarls* of King Harold Godwinsson were famously armed with such axes when their shield-wall withstood Duke William's Norman cavalry during long hours on the battlefield of Hastings in 1066.

Left: This helmet is of the most common type then in use – the *spangenhelm,* characterized by its construction from several plates riveted to a frame. The attached nasal is popularly associated with the 11th-century Normans, but in fact it is seen in many of the specimens found right across Europe. Among a number of complete helmets found are examples from Olmütz and Hainburg.

Left: The *seax* is carried here with the sharpened edge upwards, and that side of the sheath is reinforced with brass. The item hanging from the belt near the knife hilt is a fire-striking steel, used with a piece of flint to strike sparks into tinder to light a fire. The decorated copper-alloy strap end of the belt indicates the warrior's relative wealth.

A large knife is slung from the waist belt to hang horizontally across the warrior's abdomen. In the usual terminology, a 'knife' is a tool or weapon with a single sharpened edge to the blade, while a 'dagger' has both edges sharpened, tapering to the point. Throughout the medieval era knives of various sizes were the universal tools for daily work and personal cutlery at mealtimes, and were the first and indispensable item of an individual's basic equipment for everyday life. However, by late antique times this tool had already developed into a weapon of war in some Frankish regions of south-west Germany and eastern France, and this 'big knife' became a separate category called a *seax*. Finds from the turn of the 6th/7th century, with blades up to about 60cm (23.6in) long and 6cm (2.3in) broad, are not uncommon. This type of weapon may have travelled to England with the Angles and Saxons during the 'migration' period, and archaeology reveals that in the Saxon settlement areas they remained in use during most of the Viking age. The impact of a large *seax* might be compared with that of a machete.

Although body armour became more common over time, the contemporary techniques of close-quarter battle still made the shield indispensable. With a diameter of approximately 1m (40in), that carried by our reconstructed warrior looks very much the same as those of his ancestors. The body is still made from thin, narrow, planed planks, but in this case the hemispherical boss has a decorative hexagonal base; an iron grip and additional plate reinforcements are riveted to the interior, and the rim is secured by a strip of rawhide fixed with small nails.

Although sources do mention that in battle the front of Viking helmets sometimes bore a painted *herkumbl* or 'war mark', which was presumably an insignia of some kind, the colours of shields during this period seem to have been purely decorative. The fact that all the shields found in the Gokstad ship burial had been painted in either solid black or yellow does not negate this. The colours mentioned most frequently in the sources are red (often), yellow, black, white, and occasionally green or blue. It is not impossible, of course, that warriors of a certain group painted their shields in the same colours for better identification on the battlefield, but this cannot be equated with the much later use of heraldic 'arms'.

Clothing

The costume of our English-born Dane – or Danish Englishman – corresponds with late 10th-century fashion. The tunic (or 'kirtle') has increased in length over time, and now reaches to the top of the knee. It is no longer cut straight: to give the garment enough width to allow a decent length of pace on the march, gussets have been inserted into the skirt below the waist. This was necessary because the looms used to weave cloth in that period only allowed a bolt width of 80–90cm (32–36in), and cutting 'wedge' sections out of a broad panel would have

Below: The interior of the shield, with metal reinforcements. These, and the boss, are fixed not just with simple nails bent over on the inside of the planks, but by rivets with rectangular washers.

led to a waste of expensive material. Using different colours for the gussets also made the whole garment more handsome. The use of dyed fabric, and the colourful braids applied to decorate the edges, indicates a superior grade of garment. The greyish-blue colour would have been achieved by using woad (*Isatis tinctoria*) on a natural grey woollen fabric, while the Bordeaux-red can be obtained by dyeing with common madder or dyer's madder (*Rubia tinctorum*). The shirt just visible under the tunic is sewn from bleached linen and, like the trousers, is designed to meet functional needs; neither shows any decorative elements.

The equally undecorated leather shoes are of a common European type of the period, characterized by the pointed rear end of the sole being turned up behind the heel into the upper part. The term 'turn-shoe' originated in the manufacturing technique; the separate parts were sewn together over the shoemaker's 'last' with the shoe turned inside-out, and only after the sewing was finished was it turned right-side out.

Following 10th-century fashion, the waist belt is quite narrow, and decorated in the same manner as the sword baldric. Besides the pouch with tooled decoration, which probably holds a comb and razor, other items are directly strung to the belt: a fire-striker, and a grooming set consisting of tweezers and a spatula to clean the ears.

Above: The main advantage of the 'turn-shoe' technique of manufacture was that the sewn seams were securely on the inside, so did not wear out as fast as if they had been exposed on the outside.

Below: Re-enactors give an impression of a 10th- or 11th-century combat. Some have *spangenhelms*, others simpler one-piece helmets of similar shape, but both types have nasals to protect the face. Only a minority of warriors have ring-mail, and since most have to rely on padded 'soft armours' the use of shields is essential.

EX IUDEIS ET CREDEBANT IN E
EST
lectio
gelic
tisum
hodie
de qui
sumu
Quedam
tam m
ut potius auctorem qua
desiderent; In eas nos

Norman *Miles*

11th to 12th Century

Of all the colonies founded by the Norsemen before the turn of the millennium, one gave birth to an extraordinarily successful and long-lived political and military culture: Normandy.

By their prowess and the political skill of their leader, Hrolf, a Danish army that had been ravaging the Seine valley created, by the year 933, a more or less autonomous duchy for themselves within the Frankish kingdom. Hrolf took the Frankish name Rollo, and the Frankish status of *dux* or duke was inherited by his heirs. By 1100 these energetic and expansionist 'Normans' were at the summit of their power, with vigorous offshoots holding territories from Sicily in the south to Scotland in the north.

The rise of the Normans (who had soon become Frankish themselves in all but name) was supported by the development of a new warrior elite with a new fighting tactic, which for the following five centuries would dominate the European battlefield and the socio-political culture alike: the mounted, armoured 'knight'. For hundreds of years past, Western battles had been fought face-to-face, on foot; now the Normans developed a completely new technique of fighting from horseback. Now the horse was not only the fighting man's transport to the battlefield, it was trained to play an integral part in combat. Knee to knee, mounted warriors rode in closely formed blocks of up to thirty men, protected by armour and with long lances outstretched. This so-called *conroi* cavalry block had a menacing psychological effect on opponents, whose battle lines would often break at its mere advance.

While the armour of a professional soldier had always been an important cost factor limiting the size of armies, the requirements for mounting and outfitting such a knight would be even more demanding. For instance, at the end of the 11th century a normal riding horse was worth the same as five bulls, but a trained warhorse *(destrier)* cost as much as seven riding horses. At least one of these extremely expensive mounts was needed by every knight to conduct *conroi* tactics (and often a spare horse, too, if he were not to run the risk of finding himself dismounted and more or less redundant after the first combat). The tactics of these massed cavalry attacks could only succeed if every man in the formation had a similar mount and equally good equipment.

The feudal system

The economic burden of providing the resources for a sizeable cavalry force would have beggared even the wealthiest king, but the 'feudal' system established by the Normans enabled them to solve this dilemma. As practised in Normandy, in England after the Norman Conquest of 1066, and in other Norman territories acquired later, this system rested upon the doctrine that all land belonged, by the grace of God, to the king. The king granted landed estates, including ownership of the unfree peasants who worked them, to a 'pyramid' hierarchy of capable nobles and knights.

These land holdings (fiefdoms) were sufficiently productive and profitable to finance the military necessities, and in return for their estates each level of Norman society 'swore fealty' to

Right: The primary weapon for fighting in the *conroi* mounted squadron was necessarily a long-shafted pole-arm, which would give the range to strike a man in the enemy's line before the horses came too close together. The 'winged' lance illustrated is quite a good example of such a weapon; with an overall length of more than 3m (nearly 10ft), it allows a long fighting reach from horseback. It also provides a means of displaying the knight's personal pennon.

the lord above them, and thus ultimately to the king. Under the terms of this compact they bound themselves to provide fully equipped men for military service.

In the top level of this feudal pyramid, great dukes held enough territory to distribute many fiefdoms to lesser nobles and knights, thus ensuring a considerable number of retainers to support their personal efforts. (Norman kings granted these greatest men fiefs dispersed around the kingdom, so that in theory no one duke would rule a unified territory big enough to challenge the king.) At the base of the system was a large group of free men who held small fiefdoms, barely adequate to equip themselves and a handful of followers with the war gear and horses they needed when called up for a campaign. Despite these inequalities, even these ordinary knights were allowed to carry their own insignia, a pennon or personal flag usually fixed beneath the head of the lance. A fierce pride in their shared knightly status bred a culture of solidarity, irrespective of differences in personal wealth, and this could give an army a psychological resilience that might outweigh the practical difficulties they faced.

Above: This view shows the excellent protection provided by the 'kite' shield in conjunction with the helmet and mail hauberk. The padded right foream is covered to some extent by the movements of the sword, and only the lower legs are completely unprotected.

The 'kite' shield

A member of this class of mounted Norman knights was termed in Latin a *miles* ('soldier'). During the second half of the 11th century a man-at-arms like our reconstruction could have been seen serving in several other European armies as well as those of the Normans themselves, since their tactics were copied quite soon after their first successes on the battlefield, and mercenary knights travelled quite widely to rent out their services and seek their fortunes. (Typically, these were the younger sons who would not inherit lands from their fathers.)

The most immediately notable contrast from the equipment of his predecessors is the large almond- or 'kite'-shaped shield that protects his body from chin to shins. A shield of these dimensions frustrated the enemy's cuts and thrusts during hand-to-hand combat, and, when lifted and tilted back, it gave cover from the arrows that were an increasing threat on the battlefield. It still had a hemispherical iron boss, although this was now of no practical use, since there was no 'cut-out' in the shield to accommodate the fist gripping a central interior handle. To protect the edge from cuts, iron bands were now beginning to replace rawhide. On the interior of the shield three straps were riveted (*see* page 50); the forearm was passed through one of them and the second acted as a hand grip, with a pad between them to protect the forearm (which was now pressed against the wood) from the transmitted force of blows. This arrangement

Below: The linen braies normally reached to the knee. Here the separated woollen hose worn over them are untied from the laces hanging from the belt-cord of the braies and rolled down, as if in warm weather.

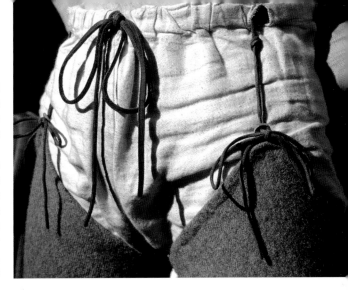

allowed the shield to be manipulated in combat, or to be carried with the arm hanging vertical without too much fatigue. The third, much longer strap *(guige)* enabled the knight to sling the shield on his back when it was not needed, and in battle it also distributed some of the weight of the shield to the shoulder.

The shield of our reconstructed *miles* is painted with the same colours and emblem as those of his lance pennon, here a white cross on a dark red ground. The iconography shows many simple blazons or patterns of this kind, and common sense argues that they were already used to identify friend from foe on the battlefield. While the practice of displaying inherited family 'livery colours' or a heraldic 'coat of arms' had yet to evolve, these early colours and emblems presumably represented an early stage of this tradition.

Above & right: The gambeson is closed by lacing up the back. This naturally requires the help of a second person when putting on the armour, but it is necessary in order to avoid a weak area at the front over the vulnerable breast. Metal buckles are unsuitable, since they would snag in the ring-mail worn over the gambeson.

Under-armour garments

Watching the reconstructed *miles* putting on his gear in the photographs gives us a good insight into the practicalities of his equipment.

The first thing to notice is that from the 11th century onwards the old Germanic-style trousers were replaced by a pair of separate 'hose' (which had the advantage that they could be rolled down to the ankles in hot weather). It was not until the 14th century that separate-leg hose once more began to be united into a single garment, and in some cases the separated hose were retained until the late 15th century. The hose were fastened by laces to the belt of a pair of wide-cut, knee-length linen drawers called *braies*. A long, loose linen shirt was worn over these, reaching below the crotch.

The padded garment worn directly over the shirt was now called a *gambeson;* it was an integral part of the body protection, absorbing the kinetic force of blows. It was knee-length, and its sleeves now extended the full length of the arm; ring-mail armour with long sleeves was only just coming into use at the end of the 11th century, though it would later become common. The edges of this padded or quilted fabric garment were reinforced with leather. The gambeson, like the mail shirt worn over it, was divided at the front and back of the skirt part so that a mounted warrior could sit his saddle comfortably, with these protective garments hanging naturally down the outside of his legs. (By contrast, long mail armour made for purely infantry use was sometimes divided

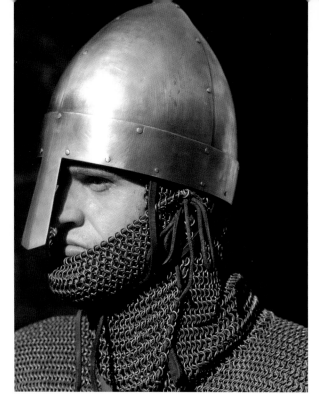

Above: To prevent the helmet from sliding about on the smooth surface of the mail hood, and to keep it steady under blows from weapons, it is held in place by strong leather laces attached at four points in front of and behind the ears. Note the necessary space between the helmet's nasal and the face – if it fitted too closely, then a sword-blow on it would break the wearer's nose.

Above: The knight puts on his mail hood with its integral face-piece; this aventail is fastened by a leather lace tied behind the left ear. Note the standing collar of the gambeson; under the hood he already wears a padded cap (*see* page 43). Together, the mail and the padding give protection against cuts and blows to the neck and lower face.

at each side, to give the legs freedom of movement without compromising the protection at the front of the groin.)

War gear

The mail shirt itself – in medieval times termed a *hauberk* – still has only short sleeves, but it now reaches down to the knees. Another innovation is that the 11th-century hauberk now has an integral ring-mail hood to give face protection, extending directly from its neckline. This hood had to incorporate extra rings to give a long, loose neck (*see* top left), and this was not only to make it easier for the warrior to turn his head freely. The weight of ring-mail is not distributed evenly over the body, but drags straight downwards from the highest point, which is usually the shoulders. If the hood had been close-fitting the head would have borne a greater part of the total weight of the armour, causing greater fatigue.

Right: A typical position while struggling to put on a ring-mail hauberk. Its construction makes it both slippery and difficult to control, since the weight constantly shifts as the wearer turns and bends his body. The most practical way is to hold it rolled up like a sweater, and then put the arms through the sleeves while bending your body forward and downwards (this is a great deal easier when a second pair of hands is available to pull the lower edge up the slope of your back). You then stand upright with raised arms, allowing the weight of the mail to slide it down your body. A helpful final step is to jump up and down a few times to settle the mail in place. Taking the hauberk off requires a reversal of this procedure, until it all drops forward under its own weight and off your arms and head.

A helmet of rounded conical shape completes the protective armour. This, the most common type seen during this period, might either be forged from one plate of steel, or formed by riveting several plates together between vertical and horizontal bands, but in either case it featured a 'nasal' as face protection.

The sword

The sword retained its importance in this era. Although the lance was the primary weapon in the charge of the mounted *conroi*, there was a high probability of it getting broken or being dropped in the first clash. It was anyway almost useless for close combat, so after the opposing sides came together the sword was a far more effective weapon.

Except in the case of Norsemen and Saxons armed with the 'broad axe' (*see* page 24), the primary weapon for opposing troops fighting on foot was a spear. This could be held overarm with the right hand at the point of balance, and thrust over and around the edge of the shield at the opponent, whose face and throat were still vulnerable even if he was wearing a ring-mail hauberk – and foot-soldiers often lacked anything better than padded 'soft armour'. At such close range, however, the more versatile sword was still the superior cut-and-thrust weapon.

Our reconstructed Norman's sword, with its fairly massive 'Brazil-nut' shaped pommel to balance the weight of the blade, and its straight guard, is of a kind typical for the late 11th century. While the sword blades of the early and middle Viking age were relatively broad with parallel cutting edges, meant for heavy cutting blows on often unarmoured targets, in the time of our *miles* blades grew longer and more pointed. This is explained by the requirement for a longer reach when fighting from horseback, as well as by the need to make thrusts, rather than cuts, against armoured enemies.

Unlike those of earlier and later centuries, the scabbard and sword belt were not ornamented: a simple chape protecting the tip of the scabbard from wear was the only metal fitting, as even the buckle of the belt was replaced by leather lacing.

Above: This reconstructed sword was made in imitation of several original examples surviving in museum collections. The pommel on the hilt, of a shape known today as the 'Brazil-nut' type, is heavy enough to counterbalance the weight of the blade when the sword is held in one hand, allowing good control of the tip. The scabbard and suspension system is of leather with virtually no metal parts, substituting careful interlacing and knotting for metal rings and buckles.

Below: Re-enactors create the impression of a clash between infantry during an 11th-century battle. The big 'kite' shields could be almost interlocked by a close rank of men, each one partly protecting the right flank of the man to his left. Here attackers (from the left of the scene) seem to have burst a gap in the 'shield-wall' of their opponents, but reinforcements hurry to close it. Shields could also be used offensively, to push or knock an opponent off balance.

Infantry Serjant

Second Half of 12th Century

For many centuries following the downfall of the Roman Empire in the West, armies in western Europe were not divided into separate 'branches of service'. Armies marched and fought on foot. The horses of the wealthier men were used for transport alone; when they reached the battlefield their riders dismounted to fight on foot, and there was no 'cavalry' to operate independently. Neither were there specialist groups using long-range weapons, differentiated from the mass of what the Roman Army had called *pedites* ('foot-soldiers'). The equipment of a warrior was totally dependent on his own financial means or those of the chieftain whom he followed, and the choice of weapons was governed by individual taste and capabilities.

(The qualification 'western Europe' is important; a professional army based, at least at first, on the old Roman model survived in the eastern or Byzantine half of the Empire, ruled from Constantinople, for a thousand years after the fall of Rome.)

As the feudal system permeated western and central European society during the 11th century, and the evolution of knighthood formed not only a new social class but also a specialized military branch, the foot-slogging mass of armies remained disorganized. The contingents of foot-soldiers who might be summoned for a limited period between seed-time and harvest, to defend their feudal lord's territory or, less often, to help ravage that of his neighbours, were largely untrained and unpaid levies. They had very varied levels of equipment, and thus of value on the battlefield; they would still be seen for centuries to come, but they would be increasingly irrelevant except in home defence. What were needed on campaign, and on the field of pitched battle, were well-trained infantry with more or less standardized equipment – to entrench and defend marching camps, to conduct sieges, and to form a steady base on the battlefield around which the mounted men-at-arms could manoeuvre. Their process of evolution would take centuries, but its first glimmerings can be traced to the 10th and 11th centuries.

In western Europe, their predecessors were the well-equipped personal guards in the paid service of Anglo-Saxon and Scandinavian kings and noblemen. During the 10th and 11th centuries these 'household warriors', or *huscarls*, formed the nucleus of the seasonal armies that were bulked up with local rural levies. Famously, at the battle of Hastings in 1066 King Harold's *huscarls* formed the core of the Anglo-Saxon army

– but it is less appreciated that Duke William's Norman army fielded considerable numbers of *serjants*. The Middle High German term *Serjant* (also *Serjent, Scharjante* or *Schargante*) denotes a professional, paid warrior in the service of a knight. Those at Hastings originated from Flanders and Brittany, and formed independent units each commanded by a knight.

Right: The serjant prepares for a training fight in the courtyard of his employer's castle. Although he is a foot-soldier he would have ridden when out about his knight's business, thus the slit in the skirt of his hauberk. Note the slight 'belly' of mail hanging over his belt; if the belt is buckled too tightly the flexibility of the mail is compromised, preventing the wearer from moving his arms freely.

War gear

The equipment of such a soldier, while neither as complete nor of as high quality as that of a member of the knightly class, would certainly be of a good standard when compared with that of the common warrior of former times, or that of the peasant levies of his own day. For reconstructing our serjant's gear we have had to rely on a few archaeological finds, some written sources, and rare paintings in books. He poses here in the courtyard of his lord's castle, perhaps ready to undertake a training session with a comrade.

Our main reason for dating him to the second half of the 12th century is his helmet. During the former centuries helmets, irrespective of their construction in one piece or several riveted sections, were of a 'conical' shape, but helmets with a rounded, bowl-shaped skull start to appear in the sources from about 1150 onwards, with the face still protected by a nasal. The iconography shows that it was not uncommon for the helmet to be coloured. The colour may have been an identification, at personal choice or that of the soldier's lord, but the idea of painting or lacquering was strictly practical. Bright steel has to be polished constantly to prevent corrosion; in a matter of hours rust will start to appear, caused by moist air or the sweat from fingerprints, and painting cuts down the need for such intensive maintenance.

Beneath his helmet our serjant is wearing only a padded cap which, together with a liner inside the helmet itself, absorbs the energy of blows. The cap is made from two layers of linen with a filling of sheep's wool in between, kept in place by seamed quilting.

The hauberk with its half-length sleeves and knee-length skirt, and the gambeson worn beneath it, resemble those worn by the *miles* in the previous chapter. The mail has probably been carefully oiled and stored in the castle's small armoury for many years, since the expense of purchasing a new hauberk would not be undertaken lightly. In contrast to his quite 'modern' helmet, the serjant's 'kite' shield is also a little old-fashioned, but no less effective for that. When a large number of men were drawn up in close order their shields formed a very durable 'wall', and if they were armed with long pole-weapons such foot-soldiers could withstand cavalry attacks.

The lance, with its 3m (10ft) shaft and 'winged' head, also has an iron ferrule at the butt end. This could be thrust into the ground at an angle and the shaft steadied with both hands, so as to absorb much more of the impetus of an enemy mounted charge than a hand-held weapon could. This long, heavy weapon is only suitable for two-handed use, in formations. For that reason the serjant also carries a sword for close-quarter fighting; its design has not changed significantly over the past century. The scabbard and belt are simple and undecorated.

Above: Round-topped helmets became common during the 12th century, as did the fashion for painting them. The lacquering helped to identify the wearer, and, more importantly, prevented rusting.

This new military type, by definition fighting only on foot, was recruited mostly from those free men who were unable, for reasons of birth and poverty, to aspire to knighthood. They took paid service with a knight or a higher member of the nobility, who provided, or at least supported the purchase of, their military equipment. (The family castle of an average knight employed, in peacetime, only a few full-time fighting men; there was usually no need for more, and their upkeep was an expense to the household.) These professionals should properly be called not warriors, but 'soldiers', since the origin of that word means precisely 'someone receiving pay'. Unlike the peasants and farmers of the general levy, they could spend most of their time training for their military calling, so they soon reached a high level of combat readiness.

Right: The gambesons made for wearing beneath armour were, while adequately padded, not so strong as the similar but unpadded garments made for use alone as 'soft armours'. Since these 'jacks' had to protect against blows, cuts and arrows they were more substantially made of multiple layers of material rather than padded quilting, though still carefully shaped to allow ease of arm-movement. A later specification issued by King Louis XI of France in *c.*1470 gives very detailed instructions for their manufacture, using twenty-five or thirty layers of cloth and one layer of stag's leather.

Clothing and utensils

Off duty and free of his armour, our serjant takes some refreshment. Coopered wooden vessels like the jug he is using, as well as tankards, food bowls and buckets, were in widespread use during the Middle Ages. (Incidentally, whatever the serjant is drinking, it is probably not water. Fermented weak or 'small' beer was the safest and most common drink for the lower classes for many centuries, since clean, potable water was seldom found in the wells and cisterns of settlements.)

The soldier's main garment is the knee-length tunic or 'kirtle' corresponding with a fashion worn until the late 14th century. As before, the fullness of the skirt is achieved by inserting wedge-shaped gussets of fabric during construction. The edges are modestly decorated by hemming with a strip of a different coloured fabric. The costume is completed by a woollen cap made from four segments sewn together, a linen shirt and a pair of woollen hose. His ankle-length shoes, secured with laces passing around the ankle, are of the common 'turn-shoe' type found on many contemporary archaeological sites.

To sum up, we might repeat that neither the military equipment nor the personal costume of the 12th-century serjant are comparable with the equivalents to be found in a knight's chambers. Clearly, everything is of practical design and quality craftsmanship – a reasonable investment of expense for a lord who needed to equip several men in the same manner. Our serjant is equivalent to a paid artisan, not a beggar or brigand; he and his family have been provided with a home that should last as long as their knight's fortunes prosper.

The abandonment of the decorative elements sported by previous warriors reconstructed in this book (for instance, metal belt- and pouch-fittings, and brightly-coloured braid on the clothing) may be a consequence of Christian belief. A good Christian was supposed to show his humility by avoiding ostentatious display – a rule that was easier to abide by at this soldier's economic level than it was for the nobility.

Above left & left: Following contemporary fashion, the personal belt kit, like the sword belt, is plain and undecorated. His pouch carries the same sort of contents as in previous times, e.g. a whetstone, fire-striker, etc. The knife sheath carried behind it (to hold the knife secure) has only a small brass chape. With a blade about 20cm (8in) long, this knife was employed for everyday use and at the table, though it could also be used as a sidearm in an emergency. A similar example was found during excavations at a castle in the Rhineland called Haus Meer.

Above right: Pottery of this kind, of a white base colour with red or red-brown geometrical or other decoration, was in widespread use at the beginning of the High Medieval period. This particular type is named 'Pingsdorfer Ware' after the best-known centre of its manufacture, the village of Pingsdorf near Cologne.

Right: A sufficient supply of water or safer drinks was not only desirable when off duty. In hot seasons especially, physical exertion while wearing the military equipment reconstructed in this book carried a real risk of heat exhaustion, and was only possible with frequent liquid refreshment. Incidentally, fragments of coopered wooden vessels made in the same way as the serjant's jug are found in such large quantities during the excavation of medieval sites that it is even possible they outnumbered similar items made of pottery.

Knight Templar of the Third Crusade, 1190

At the end of the 11th century a new era opened, which over time would come to involve most of the powers of Europe, the eastern Mediterranean, and what we call today the Middle East: the age of the Crusades.

In the mid-7th century the new religion of Islam had burst out of its cradle in Arabia, and its armies had swept northwards, eastwards and westwards to incorporate Arabs, Persians, and Turks from Central Asia, creating the Muslim world that would eventually stretch from the borders of France to those of India. In the early 8th century Muslims crossed from Morocco to Spain and soon reached the Pyrenees, where they eventually halted. During the 9th century intermittent warfare continued between the Islamic caliphates and Christian Europe, both in the West and on the borders of the Byzantine Empire, against a background of trading contacts that enriched both civilisations. The Islamic world itself was fragmented by constant internecine wars, and during the 11th century a new Muslim power split off from the Seljuk Turkish empire in Iran and Iraq. These Seljuks of Anatolia threatened the Fatimid caliphs of Egypt, and in the 1070s they also overran much of the Byzantine Empire. Putting aside the mutual suspicions that divided the Orthodox Christian East from the Roman Catholic West, the Byzantine emperor appealed to the West for help.

At the Council of Clermont in 1095, Pope Urban II called upon the leaders of European Christendom not only to help defend Byzantium against the Seljuks, but also to free the sacred sites of the Holy Land – above all, Jerusalem, the scene of Christ's Passion and Resurrection – from the Muslims. (For believing Christians, the appeal of this summons was a promise of the forgiveness of sins for those who responded; for the Pope and European sovereigns, it also offered a convenient diversion of the quarrelsome nobility of the West from endemic internal warfare.) The following year a large multi-national 'Frankish' army, accompanied by many non-combatant pilgrims, set out on long journeys for Constantinople in what became known as the First Crusade. In 1097 they landed in Syria, and defeated a Seljuk army at the battle of Dorylaeum in modern Turkey. In 1098 the Fatimids from Egypt re-occupied Palestine, which had until then been simply a buffer state between them and the Seljuks, but in 1099 the Crusaders captured Jerusalem (and subjected the population to a merciless massacre).

Over the years that followed, internal conflicts among the Muslim powers allowed the establishment by Normans and other western Crusaders of baronies in Syria and Palestine,

most of them owing feudal allegiance to an elected King of Jerusalem. It was not until 1147 that Muslim pressure on this Crusader state prompted a Second Crusade to defend it; this both suffered defeats by the Seljuks and achieved victories over the Fatimids. In 1169 Salah-al-Din ('Saladin'), a brilliant Kurdish commander serving the Seljuk sovereign Nur-al-din, seized Egypt; he himself took power after Nur-al-Din's death in 1174, and captured most of Syria. Finally, Saladin and his 'Saracen' army reconquered Jerusalem after wiping out a Crusader army at the battle of Hattin in 1187.

Right: By about the mid-12th century a red cross on the white shield, surcoat and pennon was the insignia of the Order of the Temple; in this case it is even repeated in the painting of the helmet. In 'civilian' dress the Knights Templar wore a monk's white hooded habit with the red cross on the breast, and the Order's serjants wore brown clothing with the same red cross.

The loss, once again, of the sacred sites in the Holy Land induced European monarchs to call for a Third Crusade. Under the leadership of the Emperor Frederick I 'Barbarossa' of the Holy Roman Empire, the French King Philip II Augustus, and the English King Richard I 'the Lionheart', strong armies were gathered with the aims of liberating Jerusalem and re-establishing the borders of the Crusader state. Although the first goal was not achieved by the crusaders' campaigns of 1189–91, during eventual peace negotiations King Richard persuaded Saladin to allow free access to the sacred places for all Christian pilgrims. The 13th century would see Fourth and Fifth Crusades: the former turned aside to capture and sack Constantinople, ruining the Byzantine Empire for fifty years, and neither expedition even approached success in the Holy Land. The final downfall of the Crusader state, at the hands of the Mamluks from Egypt, followed in 1291.

The Knightly Orders

These voluntary military-religious associations, bringing together knights from many nations, had a special role during the age of the Crusades. The first, the Order of the Temple, was first formed in Jerusalem in 1119 by Hugues de Payens with eight other knights. Sworn to obey an iron discipline, its members combined the military virtues of knighthood with the religious virtues of monks, for the purpose of guaranteeing safe passage to Christian pilgrims visiting the Holy Land. The name of the

Above: Stocking-like mail chausses protect the lower legs – a useful addition when fighting from horseback. Like the hose, they are suspended by laces from the waist belt of the braies.

Left: The rather crude, 'bucket'-like helmet is a precursor of the later *heaume* or 'great helm'. The nasal has now been extended into a complete, rigid face-guard. The slots for the eyes and for ventilation are much larger than those found on later developments of this style.

Order was derived from the location of their headquarters, near the ancient site of the Temple in Jerusalem. During the years that followed the Order attracted many pious knights and support from several European sovereigns, and grew into a significant military force. Another Order, that of St John of the Hospital of Jerusalem (the 'Knights Hospitaller'), began as a medical aid organization, but by the 1130s they were combining this charitable service with a military role. By the mid-12th century each of the Orders could field several hundred knights, plus many more serjants and hired local mercenaries; they garrisoned important castles, and formed the elite of the armed strength of the Crusader state.

War gear

The change that immediately catches the eye is the adoption of a long textile garment worn over the mail armour. Probably copied from the crusaders' Saracen opponents in order to protect the armour from the heat of the sun, this *surcotte* became an integral part of the warrior's costume all over Europe. A secondary advantage was that the surcoat gave the wearer another means, apart from the shield and pennon, to display insignia of his collective allegiance, such as the red cross on white of the Knights Templar. As the system of family heraldry developed in Europe over the next 150 years, the surcoat came to display an individualized 'coat of arms'.

The mid-12th century shield was a slight development of the 11th-century 'kite' shape, still of relatively large dimensions to cover the whole torso but with the top edge lowered and cut straight. The main change to the ring-mail hauberk was that it now had long sleeves, with integral mail mittens covering the backs of the hands. The palms and inside thumbs of the mittens were made of leather to give a secure grip; this leather part had a slash to allow the hand to be thrust out, so that the whole armour did not have to be taken off in order to free the hands. The legs were now also covered by ring-mail 'stockings' or *chausses*, suspended from the waist in the same way as the hose worn beneath them. There is some evidence for these being worn as early as the later 11th century, e.g. by Norman knights depicted in the famous Bayeux Tapestry, but they were now much more common. The natural tendency of mail to drag downwards made it difficult to fasten it in place on the legs; note the illustration from the 'Westminster Psalter' reproduced on page 40, which shows incomplete chausses laced together up the back of the legs over the hose.

The main development of the armour can be seen in the protection of the head. The mail *coif*, still worn over a quilted fabric cap, is now a separate piece from the hauberk, with a cape-like extension that partially doubles the mail protection over the shoulders. The helmet, now of a flat-topped cylindrical shape, has a big face-guard generously slotted for vision and breathing. This foreshadows the form of the later 'great helm' of the 13th and 14th century, in which a process of sideways extension of the face-guard completely surrounded the lower head and neck. In later years the great helm was more often used for jousting tournaments than for actual battle, and tended to have much smaller apertures for vision and ventilation.

The gambeson worn beneath the mail armour also shows some difference from its predecessors; it has a stiff, standing collar, but the main change is visible at the arms. At the shoulder/armpit area and at the elbows, where the wearer needs

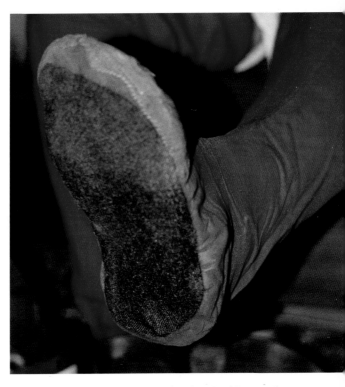

Above: The thin leather soles sewn to these hose would not stand up to walking any distance, but usefully protect the woollen material from everyday wear and tear without the need to wear shoes.

maximum flexibility, the padding is reduced, while the areas most vulnerable to an enemy's blows have additional layers of fabric for better protection.

On those occasions when they could bring the Saracens to face them in pitched battle, the crusader's only advantage – against more lightly equipped enemies mounted on more agile horses – was the sheer massive impact of their charge. Big, heavily armoured men riding big horses bred for battle, they wielded a heavy lance suitable for thrust and cut. At close quarters they used a two-edged broadsword with a blade roughly a metre (40in) long, suitable for fighting from the saddle or on foot. Our reconstructed Templar carries his weapon in a scabbard and belt made of undecorated leather; this, together with an abandonment of costly, decorated materials for 'civilian' clothing, reflects the monkish traditions of the Order (although its land holdings and treasury became extremely rich). Beneath his armour and gambeson our knight would wear linen braies and a long shirt, woollen hose and a knee-length tunic. When not dressed for war he would proudly display a Cistercian monk's long white habit (in this period only clerics or persons of high rank usually wore garments reaching to the ankle.) Against the cold he might wear a cloak of semi-circular cut.

Far left & left: The lower extension of the separate ring-mail hood doubles the layer of mail over the vulnerable base of the neck at the shoulders; the face is no longer covered with an aventail, since it is protected by the helmet's face-guard. Naturally, a padded hood is still worn under the mail.

Left & above: Note the arrangement of the shield's forearm- and grip-straps, and its sling. The broad-bladed sword, with a 'Brazil-nut' pommel and curved guard, is 'Type XII' according to Oakshott's system of classification (*see* Bibiliography). Scabbard and suspension are completely made from leather, and undecorated.

Above: This knee-length gambeson, slit for wear on horseback, shows typical sweat-staining. Note that parts which must bend easily, e.g. at the shoulders and elbows, are thinly quilted, in contrast to the heavier padding elsewhere.

Below: Re-enactors recreate a skirmish between 12th-century crusaders and Saracens.

Castellan Knight and Foot-Soldier

Late 12th Century

The most visible sign of feudal society was the castle – not just a fortified home for the nobleman or lesser knight, but an instrument and symbol of his power over the surrounding countryside. The commander of a castle was known as a *castellan*.

Until about AD1000 the wealthy elite of Europe lived in manors, which we may imagine as large farmsteads. They were surrounded by earth ramparts, ditches, and/or timber palisades to protect the inhabitants and their livestock from robbers and wild animals, but these could not be considered as having a true military function like the defences of the old Roman forts. The term 'castle', from the Latin *castellum* meaning a fortified place, was used of any natural defensive position that could provide protection for the inhabitants of the surrounding area in times of danger. It implied the addition of ramparts, palisades and gate structures in those places on the perimeter that were most vulnerable to attackers. However, 'castles' in this sense had few, if any, internal buildings for permanent occupation; since it was seldom necessary to make use of these refuges, the simplest structures were sufficient. Exceptions were the larger trading centres, which were normally protected by tall ramparts topped with palisades, wide moats, guarded gates and other fortifications. Some cities in formerly Roman areas simply used what remained of the old city walls and other, mostly public stone structures.

When Norman leaders gave populated territories to their deserving followers as feifdoms, it was necessary for the land-holders to fortify their homes – many among their new underlings and neighbours remained hostile for years, and the Normans had to anticipate attacks. William I began to erect castles immediately after his victory at Hastings, and they proliferated all over the country during his subsequent conquest of England.

These first Norman castles were small structures of a simple design which would stay in use for several hundred years. They consisted of a multi-storey timber tower built on an artificially raised or improved mound or hillock, with a palisade surrounding the foot of the mound; where the earth was dug out to form the mound a moat was developed, and adjoining the mound on level ground an outer yard was also surrounded with palisades. The tower was the residence of the knight; additional timber houses for his followers, servants and guests were built in the yard, together with workshops, stables and stores. This type of castle is called a 'motte and bailey'; the French term *chateau a motte* translates as 'castle of earth-clods', and the 'bailey' was the outer yard. Motte-and-bailey castles were still being built in some regions of Europe as late as the beginning of the 15th century, but by that time most had long been replaced by stone-built towers and walls of more impressive dimensions and design.

After the initial phase of occupation regional lords continued to build castles at points of strategic value, with good lines of sight all round. Favoured sites were on spurs of high ground that could only be approached from one direction, or dominating river crossings, major roads, and the mouths of valleys running into the hills.

Right: Standing in front of the moat of his newly erected motte-and-bailey castle, the knight feels the cutting edges of his sword.

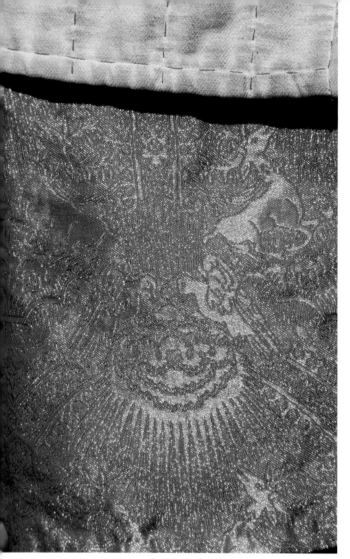

with an integral hood, and the conical helmet with a nasal, are still the predominant parts of his equipment. However, a closer look reveals certain details which remind us that fashions did not stand still.

Particularly eye-catching is the gorgeous silk gown with its woven decoration of silver brocade. Fabrics of this type were imported over long distances, probably from Byzantium or Persia and ultimately, via the 'Silk Road', from China. Perhaps our knight has returned after following his leige lord on crusade, and has been awarded his feifdom in reward for his loyalty and courage during a campaign in the Holy Land? The very length of this garment is itself a clear sign of wealth. During this period the male upper garment usually did not reach below the knee, and those extending almost to the ground were unmistakable signs of high social status.

Another expensively fashionable item is his highly decorated shield, here slung on his back; still large enough to cover most of the torso, it already has a straight-cut top. The display of identifying symbols or coloured patterns, simply assumed by an individual rather than regulated by any authority, was well established by the late 12th century. Here much care has been put into the colourful decoration of the shield; bright colours like these required pigments made out of powdered crystals or rare earths, only obtainable by long-range trade and therefore quite expensive. By using a base medium made with linseed oil or egg-white it was possible to get a durable, colourful finish with these pigments. While most of the field is lacquered in a bright blue, perhaps made from the minerals Ultramarine or Azurite, the yellow tone could be achieved with common Ochre, while the green decorations may be painted with a pigment made from Italian 'Green Earth'.

The straps of the shield allow it to be carried securely on the left arm, with the arm slipped through the short lower strap and the hand gripping the junction of the upper 'X'-straps, while a thick pad protected the forearm from impacts transmitted through the wood from blows on the outside face. Again, the long guige allowed the shield to be slung on the back for travelling, or could also be used in battle by the knight when he was mounted. With the strap looped over his head to his right shoulder, it suspended the shield to protect the left side of his body, which faced towards the enemy. This left both his hands free to steady a heavy lance rather than simply 'couching' it under his right arm. All the straps are fixed with rivets that protrude through the boards of the shield and engage metal washers.

Once again, the hooded ring-mail hauberk is worn over a padded linen cap and a gambeson, and covers most of the body except for the face. Like the crusader's legs on pages 41–45,

During the 12th and 13th centuries castles grew in size; most often the outer bailey was incorporated into the central structure, with additional buildings. Baileys still outside the central structure were secured with additional battlemented 'curtain' walls, and smaller towers spaced along them for all-round observation. Step by step, the typical castle developed around these courtyards; some survive today, whole or in still-impressive ruins, and these much-visited attractions epitomize most people's ideas about the medieval epoch.

We meet our knight at some time around the year 1175, in the bailey of his newly erected motte in a still potentially hostile part of England. The mound of sod as yet shows hardly any growth of grass and weeds, the timber of the construction is still fresh, and while the moat has filled with water from a nearby stream the additional palisade is still missing. As he inspects progress, the knight apparently thinks it worthwhile to wear his full armour.

Clothing and war gear

At first sight this knight does not look very different from those who fought with his grandfather on Senlac Hill near Hastings more than a hundred years previously. The ring-mail hauberk

Left: Details of the interior of the shield, with straps and forearm pad. It is coloured red using an iron-oxide paint.

Below: The mace carried at the hip as a secondary hand-to-hand weapon.

the knight's are protected by separate ring-mail chausses, but this time they are completed with mail feet. The chausses are suspended from an inner belt, and held securely in place by leather straps below the knees and laces at the ankles. On his feet are the most important public sign of his knightly status apart from his sword: the spurs, presented to him when he was knighted by his leige lord – thus the phrase 'earning your spurs'.

The helmet

While his shield is, as we might say, *'à la mode'* , our knight's helmet is a little old-fashioned. The conical shape with the narrow nasal is more or less identical to those worn a century before, of a design already being replaced by round-topped helmets, or flat-topped helms with complete faceguards. However, it took many years for one style to completely replace another: in manuscripts such as the famous mid-13th century 'Maciejowski Bible' we still see both conical and round-topped helmets with nasals, and completely enclosed helms, being worn

Right: Simple prick-spurs of this type, made from a copper alloy, were in use in Central Europe from ancient times until the 13th century, when they began to be replaced by rowel-spurs. They are held in place by leather straps around the insteps; note, too, the laces securing in place the ankle and foot sections of the mail chausses.

Right: 'Phrygian'-shaped steel helmet, worn over the integral mail hood of the hauberk. Obscured here is the triangular flap of mail that was drawn across the chin and up to fasten behind the left ear – *see* photo on page 32.

together in the same painting. This knight's helmet is made from a single steel plate that was repeatedly heated, hammered, and reheated as it was 'drawn down' over a series of shaping-stakes until the correct depth was achieved. Note the slight forwards tilt of the apex, in the so-called 'Phrygian' style often seen in 12th-century sources.

The mace

Another novelty is a third weapon in addition to his heavy lance and long sword: a mace. Mounted on a hardwood shaft about 80cm (30in) long is a socketed, cast-bronze head with four pyramidal projections from a cubic base; in this case the shaft has painted decoration similar to that on the border of the shield. Often the bronze head was cast as a hollow form and then filled with lead, to give additional weight and thus increased force to the blow.

This simple but effective weapon – a lethally advanced version of the most primitive club – came into use particularly by mounted warriors during the 11th century. Since heavy helmets and body armour were then being used by an increasing proportion of fighting men, warriors were increasingly protected against sharp blades, but a mace like this example could inflict serious crushing injuries even to an armoured man. The impact of a heavy blow concentrated into the tiny area at the tip of one of the 'pyramids' could break bones and cause other blunt-force

trauma, disabling the victim even where the cut of a sword would have limited effect.

It has been suggested that maces were adopted in imitation of the Saracens encountered during the Crusades, and hammer-like weapons were certainly widely used in the Middle East. However, there is also evidence for their use in Europe well before the First Crusade, especially by members of the 'Church militant'. A wilful misinterpretation of the Biblical injunction 'He that lives by the sword shall perish by the sword' led belligerent clerics to argue that since a mace was not a sword, they would not endanger their souls by using one. Famously, William the Conqueror's brother Odo, Bishop of Bayeux, is shown in the Bayeux Tapesty wielding a mace at the battle of Hastings.

Left: Our castellan's sword is typical of the late 12th century, with a pointed blade approximately a metre (40in) long, a 'Brazil-nut' pommel and a straight guard. In this period scabbards, belts and suspension straps were undecorated and made entirely of leather. This example, of relatively thin leather, has been stitched along the edges to reinforce them.

THE FOOT-SOLDIER

Although very similar in appearance to the knight reconstructed on the previous pages, details of this man's equipment indicate that he is a foot-soldier and not a member of the knighthood: the absence of spurs, and of the leg protection needed by a mounted man. Nonetheless, his helmet, ring-mail, sword and shield suggest that he is in the employment of a lord, or of a city, with considerable resources.

In the growing cities of High Medieval times, which gradually acquired an increasing degree of self-government independent of the feudal lords of the countryside around them, military duties were obligatory for all able-bodied citizens in times of external threat. Depending upon their social status and wealth, each class of citizens had to purchase weapons and protective gear as specified for their income group, and the inhabitants of each quarter of the town were assigned to defend a particular gate-tower

Left: A long lance or spear was an effective defensive weapon for those manning the walls of a castle or fortified town, allowing them to thrust down at climbing attackers before these could use their own weapons efficiently. The now nearly triangular shield, still large enough to cover the torso from shoulders to thighs, is painted with the colours of his leige lord or his city.

Below: Gambeson, braies, hose and shoes. 'Turn-shoes' like these have been found at many archaeological sites, discarded in garbage pits or latrines; this indicates that shoes were a kind of 'consumable' that were frequently replaced.

Above: Unlike the knight on previous pages, this foot-soldier has a helmet of 'Phrygian' shape constructed of separate plates joined by riveted bands. Manuscript illustrations show some examples of such helmets with face-guards, pierced with vision slots and ventilation holes.

and the adjoining part of the circuit of the city walls. This burden was generally accepted, since each family's lives and possessions depended upon the successful collective defence of the town.

In addition to this individual procurement, the councils of wealthy merchants who governed cities soon started to invest money in public armouries, stocked with military equipment that could be issued at need to those who could not afford their own. The 14th and 15th centuries would bring more effective missile weapons, such as crossbows and then handguns, and the purchase and upkeep of these were naturally more expensive than paying blacksmiths and carpenters to provide simple pole-arms. Over the centuries the defence militias of the separate city quarters sometimes developed into associations of armed citizens, though the character of these 'brotherhoods' changed over time. (With the more widespread availability of firearms, they would evolve into the shooting societies whose descendants still exist in some continental European communities. Naturally, though they proudly trace their historical links with those early associations for civic defence, today these are simply sporting and social clubs.)

Another development, as the years passed and weapons and tactics became increasingly sophisticated, was for cities to hire men-at-arms and complete mercenary companies of professional soldiers to defend them. If a city was wealthy enough to do this, the burghers often preferred the expense to risking their own lives and limbs. However, it was a solution that might bring its own problems: mercenaries might be unruly employees, especially if their pay was late.

Clothing

Our reconstructed foot-soldier or armoured citizen is dressed in the common clothing of the period, which showed no real difference between military and civil costume. Under a long shirt and above linen braies he wears a pair of woollen hose, fixed to the belt of the braies by textile bands or leather laces. In summer a simple 'kirtle' tunic made of linen or thin woollen cloth would have been worn as the only upper garment.

The 'turn-shoes' he wears are of a common type found at numerous archaeological sites. The method of fabrication was for the shoe to be sewn together from its separate parts while inside-out; it was then soaked in water to make it flexible, and then turned outside-in. This helped to protect the seams from rapid wear, but in general medieval shoes do not seem to have been very durable. As the process of 'turning' demanded quite thin soles, hard use soon wore holes in these. Although a type with an additional outer 'wearing-sole' were already being made

Below: The hand being slipped out of the palm-slit in the leather part of the ring-mail mitten, to perform some task demanding dexterity.

in the 13th century, the simple turn-shoe remained in use until the 15th century. It was at the beginning of the 16th century that the technique of 'frame sewing' superseded the older methods, allowing the manufacture of longer-lasting footwear.

War gear

When summoned to defend his castle or town, the soldier or militiaman put on a protective fabric cap and a padded gambeson, either quilted or more simply sewn from several overlaid layers of linen. Over this, our man's ring-mail hauberk conforms to the standards of his day. It still has the older style of integral mail hood, but also long sleeves with attached mittens. The inner part of these is made from leather, to guarantee a securer grip of his weapons than would be possible with the 'slippery' ring-mail. The leather palms are slit, to allow him to pull his hands upwards and then slip them outside the mittens when he needs his fingers free to perform such tasks as fastening buckles or knotting laces. Leather laces around the wrists keep the mittens in place at other times.

His head is protected by a conical-shaped helmet, but instead of the outdated narrow nasal of past centuries this now has an extensive face-guard. These face-guards cannot be called a medieval 'invention', since in Roman times the parade helmets worn by cavalrymen had anthropomorphic metal masks covering the whole face; 6th-century Swedish helmets from Vendel have cruder versions of the same feature, as does the 7th-century Anglo-Saxon example from the Sutton Hoo ship burial. However, in Central Europe this technique was only rediscovered

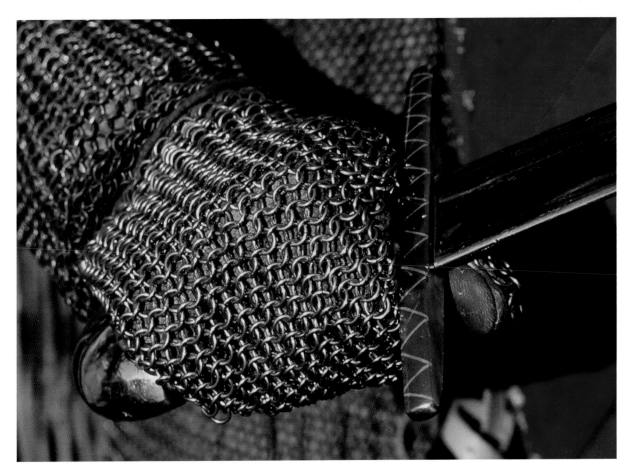

in the 12th century. During the 13th century additional armour plates were added to helmets of this type at the sides and back of the neck, as the 'great helm' gradually evolved.

Weapons

As well as a long-shafted lance, here with a winged head, he carries a two-edged sword with a straight guard and a relatively large semi-circular pommel. As always, this not only prevents his hand slipping off the end of the grip, but acts as a counterweight to balance the long blade. A well-balanced sword was a great advantage in battle: not only did it allow the blade to be manipulated with some precision, but it greatly reduced the strain on the swordsman's wrist.

As in former centuries, the sword was not carried from the waist belt but always had a separate suspension system. (The waist belt did have an important function, however; if adjusted precisely enough, preferably by a second person while the wearer stretched his arms upwards, it transferred some of the weight of the ring-mail armour from the shoulders to the hips, without compromising its flexibility over the body.) The sword belt, made from soft leather, was permanently fixed to the scabbard with leather laces. The design of the scabbard and its suspension system is shown in detail in several contemporary paintings, and there are also some surviving original pieces, thus making accurate reconstruction possible.

The development of the medieval sword over the centuries, with different types of blades in combination with different

Above: Swords were a symbol of social status, and were often inherited from father to son. The blades were manufactured by specialist smiths, and might be imported; the pommel and guard were added later by a local blacksmith, using locally influenced designs for the mounting and decoration.

designs of pommel and guard, has been analysed in some detail. The best-known scientific essay on the subject was written by the English scientist Ewart Oakeshott; his work was based on the research of the Norwegian Dr Jan Petersen, who produced the first typology of the European sword. According to their classification, the sword of our reconstructed foot-soldier is a good example of 'Type X'. Swords of this type have a blade with more or less parallel cutting edges and only a short, rounded point. Being designed primarily for delivering cutting blows, they became less effective as body armour became more common in the ranks of armies. This led to the development of tapering blades with sharper points, still suitable for cuts but also for effective thrusts to burst through the rings of mail armour.

During the High Middle Ages the technique of sword-fighting became more complex. In the course of the 14th–15th centuries sword hilts would become longer so that they could be used with a two-handed grip (contemporaries called these 'long swords', and historians call them 'hand-and-a-half' swords). Sword-fighting gradually developed from a relatively straightforward business of either slashing or stabbing into an elaborated technique that we might call 'fencing', but which had none of the delicacy which that term sometimes implies (*see pages 94–95*).

Knight and Foot-Soldier

13th to 14th Century

The term 'knight' comes from the Old English *cnight,* for a young servant as well as a warrior, and the German origin *Knecht* has the same double meaning. In other languages the derivation is much more direct: the French *chevalier,* the German *Ritter,* the Italian *cavaliere,* and the Spanish *caballero* all mean 'a horseman'. While the knight was primarily identified simply as a mounted warrior, over the centuries the term became inseparable from a particular level in society. As already explained, for economic reasons the armoured, mounted warrior was most often a land-holder, who was sworn to provide military service to a lord higher in the feudal hierarchy. Thus, by the 12th century, the knighthood of the European kingdoms had already come to form a distinct social class, who are today the iconic representatives of the Middle Ages.

This class acquired a distinct profile, separated from others by its own rites and code of behaviour. The moral code to which the knightly class aspired (though many fell far short of it in practice) was the concept of Christian 'chivalry', which encompassed all aspects of life. Besides those qualities of direct military relevance – bravery, loyalty and steadfastness – the educated Christian knight was also expected to display humility and cordiality, to respect the social hierarchy and the Church, and to protect the helpless. A central element of this intellectual world was the idealized concept of 'courtly love' for a lady. The best-known poet in this lyric tradition of the High Medieval era was a man known as Walther von der Vogelweide, whose life's work was published shortly after his death in 1230 in the form of an illuminated manuscript. This book gives us not only the chance to read chivalric poetry from a more or less contemporary source, but to see the poet himself and other knights mentioned in the text depicted in several detailed illustrations. These are an extremely important source for the reconstruction of knightly equipment, showing some of the changes that took place during the 13th century.

The 'great helm' and *cervellière*

The most obvious of these changes were to the helmet. Our reconstructed south German knight of the mid-13th century now has a *heaume* ('great helm' or 'pot helm') that fully encloses his

head and neck. This was a necessary response to developments in fighting techniques.

For example, the practice of charging with the lance braced ('couched') under the right armpit, instead of holding it in both hands, transferred more energy to the impact of the tip of the lance-head, and thus inflicted more devastating injuries. In reaction to this development protective armour was reinforced, and (as already illustrated) the face, previously more or less exposed, was now covered by a steel-plate guard. However, this first step towards the development of the 'great helm' was still made of vertical, rounded plates (*see* pages 42–43), and this left it vulnerable, particularly to vertical blows to the top delivered

Right: A fully equipped knight of the second half of the 13th century. His body and limb armour, still consisting of ring-mail only, covers him from hands to feet; it is mostly obscured (and protected from extremes of weather) by a full-cut coloured surcoat bearing his heraldic emblem. His 'great helm' completely encloses his head and neck, making him an anonymous 'iron man'. The shield, now noticeably smaller, gives less protection but can be manipulated more easily in battle. His broadsword tapers to a point, allowing thrusts that can burst through an opponent's ring-mail by breaking a few rings apart at the point of contact.

Left: The ring-mail hood was still worn beneath the great helm, although the latter covered the whole head. Here the mail aventail normally protecting the face hangs loose; note the laces to secure it when it is drawn across the lower face and up to the ear.

great helm, but in some cases as the only head protection (*see* pages 64–65), in the interests of good all-round vision when on the march, so mail face-protection was still important. The great helm itself was fixed onto the head by leather or fabric straps, and had substantial padding inside the top. This was necessary not only as a shock-absorber, but also – by means of the pad's 'doughnut' shape – to hold the helm steady over the rounded surface of the cervellière or mail hood. It needed to be secure enough that a blow would not tip it and prevent the knight seeing through the vision slots, while still allowing him to move his head freely without the helmet resting on his shoulders.

Limb armour

Protection for the arms was still provided only by the ring-mail sleeves of the hauberk worn over the gambeson, and for the hands by the attached leather-palmed mittens, but the protection of the knight's legs, which were especially vulnerable to attacks by

with heavy pole-weapons. Contemporary pictures, such as those to be found in the 'Maciejowski Bible' painted in about the year 1250, show helmets being cut in half with a single blow. (While the central image in the painting on page 80 is fantastically exaggerated, it clearly implies that armour could not always prevent catastrophic injury.)

To correct this design flaw the helmet was enlarged, at first still with vertical sides, but in later 13th-century models with sloped upper sides that gave the helmet a more tapered appearance. During this process the side and rear plates were also extended, so that the head and neck were finally completely enclosed. Additionally, the face part of the helmet was reinforced with a cross shape of extra steel bands.

Beneath the great helm the knight still wore a ring-mail hood over a padded cap. Most often the mail hood was a separate piece, but hoods integral to the mail shirt were still worn. Even the laced-across aventail on the hood was still in use, despite the face being completely covered when wearing the great helm. This was due to the fact that most often a second plate helmet was also worn: a small steel skull-cap called a *cervellière,* fastened on top of the mail hood. This was normally worn beneath the

Right: The protection worn on the legs, normally covered by other elements of the costume. The white drawers are the linen braies; on top of them and suspended from a belt are black woollen hose. On top of these, and suspended in the same way, are the ring-mail chausses, secured by leather straps and laces at the knee and ankle, and extending over the top part of the foot. The knight's spurs are attached by straps passing under the instep. On his right upper leg padded cuisses, made from quilted linen in the same way as the gambeson, are also suspended from the belt and laced at the bottom. Sewn to this fabric is a rudimentary knee protector of hardened leather.

foot-soldiers, was improved over time. Ring-mail chausses had come into use at the latest by the late 11th century. In addition to being suspended from an internal belt like the woollen hose worn under them, they were secured by leather straps or laces at the knee and ankles to prevent them from twisting around, and to relieve some weight from the belt – a not unimportant detail, as the mail stocking for each leg weighed 5–6kg (11–13lb). These chausses were open at the bottom of the foot, kept in place by leather laces criss-crossing the sole of the shoe worn beneath. To allow easier dressing a slit was left in the mail up the back of the ankle, closed by a lace when all was in place.

As additional protection, padded textile defences for the thigh and knee are mentioned from about the year 1240 onwards. These *cuisses* were made like the gambeson, with a padding material such as wool, felt or horsehair quilted in between two layers of fabric. Over these, the kneecaps might have additional protectors *(poleyns)* made from horn, hardened leather or metal.

Heraldic identification

At first sight, the equipment of this knight in the later 13th century is not very different from that of his predecessors of a hundred

Below: The foot part of the ring-mail chausses is open at the bottom, apart from a slight cap effect at the toe. It is held secure by leather laces passed through rings around the edges, and criss-crossing under the sole of the shoe worn beneath it.

Left: The 13th-century knight at rest. Note the thick padding inside the top of the great helm, both to absorb the shock of blows and to help hold it steady over the mail hood or plate skull-cap. A loop of the sword belt was fixed in position, wound around the top of the scabbard; to judge by some archaeological finds, the leather used was of a buckskin type, since most other leathers would have been too rigid. Belts were wide, to ensure stability; traditionally they were fastened with two tongues cut in the loose end of the belt, drawn through two holes in the other end and then knotted together.

Right: Now showing some of the improvements introduced in the early 14th century, this knight has a coat-of-plates and plate greaves, and flamboyantly displays his goat symbol not only on his shield but also as a three-dimensional crest attached to his helm. The crest most often echoed a major element of the heraldic arms such as a real or mythical beast, but there were no fixed rules. It could also reflect the wearer's place in society; for example, several bishops are shown in miniature paintings wearing a mitre-shaped crest on their helms.

years before, but one aspect is obvious: the display of a striking personal or family emblem. With a completely enclosed helmet the knight was now anonymous on the battlefield, so the art of heraldry had become more sophisticated. By the mid-13th century what would develop into 'coats of arms' were being worn extensively by knights and the lesser nobility, and in France and Germany the practice was even allowed among the *bourgoisie* and *Burghers* of cities. This knight's goat emblem is sewn to his surcoat (which also serves to protect his armour from hot sun or damp).

The heraldic symbol is also painted on the shield. Now rather smaller than in previous generations, this 'heater' shield (so-called by 19th-century historians from its resemblance in shape to an old-fashioned clothes-iron) was made from several criss-crossing layers of thin wooden strips, pressed and glued into its slightly bowed form. The surface was covered with leather or linen, as additional reinforcement and as a base for painting the desired pattern.

In the photos on pages 61–65 we can see some late 13th-century/early 14th-century improvements which will lead, in their turn, to a major transformation of armour during the coming decades.

The coat-of-plates

The most important of these was, again, a response to the increasing piercing-power of weapons, both hand-held and projectile. This additional protection worn over the ring-mail hauberk was termed a 'coat-of-plates'. At first glance it resembles a simple fabric surcoat, but in fact it is a kind of T-shaped, pull-over leather vest with a central hole for the head to pass through, and with a number of medium-sized steel plates riveted to its inside surface. This 'coat' protected the whole torso, with large flaps passing round the sides from front to back and buckling together at the rear. Some of these armours were hip-length, others had extensions hanging down to protect the groin. This additional defence greatly increased the protection, not only in providing a substantial extra layer of metal that increased the energy required for a weapon to pierce it, but also in that the rigid plates distributed the energy of the impact over a larger surface area of the body than was the case with mail.

The photographs on the following pages show the details of the construction of this body armour. The individual steel plates were each shaped to fit in a specific place and fixed by rivets to the leather base layer, slightly overlapping at the edges. To give the best possible protection an optimal fit had to be achieved, so ideally a coat-of-plates would have been 'made to measure' for a specific wearer. The armour was closed at the back by buckled straps and/or knotted laces. Over the leather and plates a decorative outer covering layer might be added, of linen, velvet, or (if the owner was rich and ostentatious enough) even of costly imported silk. An internal lining was not necessary, since the coat-of-plates was meant to be worn directly over the mail hauberk.

The Visby graves

Our ability to reconstruct coats-of-plates with some confidence is due to a unique opportunity to study a relatively large number of original examples recovered from a single archaeological site. This precious discovery was made in mid-13th century mass graves near Visby, once an important trading centre on the Swedish island of Gotland. When excavated between 1905 and 1930 these pits yielded the skeletal remains of nearly 1,200

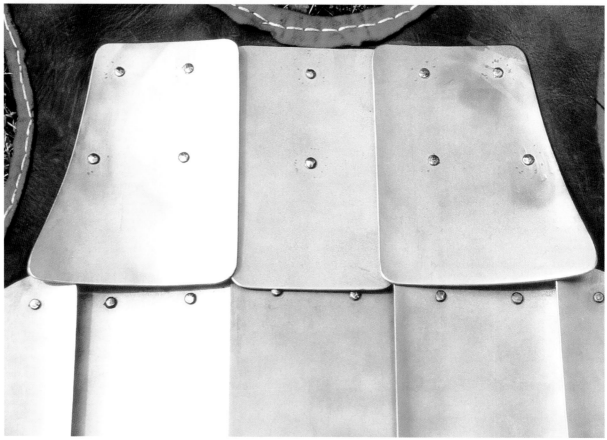

individuals, many of them showing evidence of wounds that has greatly increased our knowledge of medieval combat. Many of the skeletons in the three excavated mass graves were still wearing ring-mail hoods and, in more than 20 cases, coats-of-plates or lamellar armours.

The dead in these graves fell in battle on 27 July 1361, when the inhabitants of Visby tried to defend their town against an invading Danish army led by King Valdemar IV. The defenders were mostly untrained levies, ranging from young boys to old men (some of them even crippled, to judge from their bones), and the decisive defeat that followed cost the lives of more than 1,500 of them. Almost invariably, the dead on a medieval battlefield were carefully stripped of their valuable armour before being buried or burned, but in the perhaps unique case of Visby circumstances prevented this. By the time it was possible to clear up the battlefield several days later, we may speculate that the heat of summer had made it a revolting task carrying the threat of disease. At any rate, the bodies were

Left, above: Due to its rear fastening, the coat-of-plates can only be put on with the help of a second person. Here the side flaps are being brought backwards around the body; the narrow vertical steel plates inside these are clearly visible, and when the flaps are buckled together these protect the lower back. Some armours of this type also had plates lining the upper back to protect the shoulder blades, as clearly shown on a carved pew in Verden Cathedral.

Left, below: The interior plates of the torso, arranged in horizontal rows to give the wearer more flexibility of movement. The rivets are confined to the upper half of each plate, so that when the wearer bends forwards the leather facing of the bottom half also bends. Note the stitched edges of the external layer of red fabric over the leather.

Above: Here we see the fastening of the coat-of-plates; the rear flaps are buckled together over the unarmoured lower back of the leather vest, and the top buckle is then laced to the upper back to support the weight of the steel-lined flaps.

Left: The legs are now protected with quilted cuisses over mail chausses above the knees, hardened leather discs over the kneecap, and steel plate greaves over the chausses below the knees.

unceremoniously tipped into large grave pits complete with much of their war gear.

The wear-and-tear recognizable on the armours found at Visby, together with traces of repairs, clearly show that they had been in use for a long time before 1361. Two were made from 550–600 small, narrow iron strips *(lamellae)* laced directly together rather than riveted to a backing; this lamellar armour can be dated, by comparison with finds from other sites, to the 11th century, indicating some 200 years of use. Most of the recovered armours were coats-of-plates, of five identifiable types; these showed wide variations of detail, both in the size and positioning of the plates and in the methods of fastening. Only a few mailshirts were found, but nearly 200 separate mail hoods. None of the hauberks were found in conjunction with coats-of-plates, perhaps suggesting that the townspeople had to share around the relatively few armours they possessed.

Above: Wearing a steel helm over a cervellière, a mail hood and a quilted cap makes the head extremely hot, and the man-at-arms needed to be able to breathe freely. The asymmetrical distribution of ventilation holes on the front of this helm is due to the fact with the lance held under the right arm it is the left side that is normally exposed to an opponent. More piercings on that side of the helmet would have weakened the structure, perhaps allowing the impact of a lance to rupture it by making a crack between adjacent holes.

Helmets and limb armour

The early 14th century saw further development of the great helm. It increased in width, and instead of a reinforcing cross on the face-guard it had a sharp mid-rib intended to deflect thrusts to the sides without transmitting too much kinetic energy to the helmet, and therefore to the neck of the wearer. The piercings to allow air to ventilate the helmet were now concentrated on the right side, giving the left side – which normally faced a mounted enemy, above the edge of the shield – additional strength.

The vision slots allowed quite a good view to the sides, but only limited vision at upwards or downwards angles, since the face-guard was several centimetres in front of the eyes. This meant that the greatest threat to a mounted man was posed by foot-soldiers with pole-arms who managed to get up close.

Our reconstructed knight on pages 64 and 65 still wears a cervellière and a separate ring-mail hood beneath the great helm. The rectangular flaps hanging down from the front and back of the hood were a feature particular to the German regions.

The final element of up-armouring adopted by the early 14th-century knight was on his lower legs. While most still relied on the ring-mail chausses, some started additionally protecting the shins with plate *greaves* fastened with straps behind the calf. The spurs were still the main sign of knighthood apart from the sword. In medieval times a squire – a well-born youth who served a knight as his servant while being brought up and trained within his household, until he passed the necessary tests – aspired to be 'knighted' in a formal ceremony, when in an outward sign of his new status he had his sword girded on and his spurs buckled to his feet.

The small, rectangular plaques fixed at the shoulders in the photos on pages 64 & 65 were called in Norman French *ailettes* ('little wings'), and in German *Achsel-Schilde* ('axle-shields'). Painted with the knight's heraldic emblem, their main function is to make him identifiable to men on either side of him in battle. Some sources also ascribe to them a protective function, pointing out that they might deflect from the shoulders cuts that were glancing down off the helmet, but their position and their light materials seem quite inappropriate for this purpose. While it was normal for new developments in armour design to spread rapidly throughout the unified culture of Christian Europe, the use of ailettes in about 1275–1350 was common in France, but in Germany was limited to regions such as Westphalia, Hesse and the Rhineland.

Increasing weight, increasing exertion

Added together, the elements of a knight's protective armour now weighed not less then 30kg (70lb) carried 'on the man', with the addition of the shield and weapons. To carry

Left: Normally a skull-cap or cervellière, a firmly fitting hemispherical helmet, was worn beneath the great helm. Since it was lighter, and gave superior vision and hearing, it was also often worn without the helm.

this weight while enduring the physical exertion of a battle demanded a strong constitution, an active way of life, and thorough training and practice. However, the weight alone was not the main problem – that was the fact that as knightly equipment developed it acquired more and more layers, which increased the problem of ventilation. Even for a strong and healthy man, wearing this gear while moving vigorously for any length of time under summer conditions (even a Central European summer) brought a real danger of overheating and exhaustion.

Additionally, the monarchs and armies of the day still faced the age-old problem of expense. On the one hand, every improvement to his equipment increased the knight's protection and thus his aggressiveness in combat. On the other, each improvement demanded that more funds be invested to keep up with this progress, steadily reducing the proportion of the knighthood who could afford to maintain the latest standards.

Above: This view shows the helm decorated with a crest, carved or moulded from some light material such as boiled leather. Note the rectangular flap of the mail hood, the ailettes, the hanging mittens at the end of the mail sleeves, and the divided hanging flap of the coat-of-plates.

Left: This plainly furnished dagger might be used as a back-up weapon in case the lance or sword were lost, or not practically usable – for example, inside a building. Previously sidearms such as knives had not formed part of the knight's regular military equipment, but during the 13th century a special form of knife, the dagger, increasingly came into use by all classes of fighting men. As explained earlier, the distinction between a 'knife' and a 'dagger' is not merely semantic, but technical. The former is primarily an asymmetric everyday cutting tool with one edge sharpened; the latter is symmetrical, with two sharpened edges tapering to a sharp point, and is intended as a stabbing weapon for hand-to-hand combat.

THE FOOT-SOLDIER

During the two centuries after the first millennium the knightly heavy cavalry was always positioned in the centre of an army's battlefield array. Foot-soldiers were regarded as 'auxiliary' personnel of secondary importance, useful mainly for providing labourers and garrisons. However, this situation started to change during the 13th century, especially in the increasingly prosperous European cities. From the 11th century onwards the importance of these centres – at first economic and then, in consequence, political – had been growing as a result of far-reaching trade. Such examples of commerce as the wool trade, with raw material crossing from England to Flanders and finished clothing being distributed across the continent, and the trade in salted fish between seaports and the interior, had now reached an industrial scale.

With wealth came political influence, and a development of the towns' military abilities. The relationships between cities and the feudal nobility in whose territories they lay began to change. Originally the landholders equipped and provided men-at-arms to guarantee the safety of their properties. Now the booming cities demanded, and over time obtained (though not without struggles) greater rights of self-government. To this end they employed men-at-arms as city guards to supplement the citizen militia, and some even formed leagues of cities allied for mutual defence.

One example of a city's success in confronting the feudal nobility was the battle at Courtrai (Kortrijk), a town in modern Belgium, in July 1302. An army of French knights under the command of Count Robert II of Artois were sent there to crush a rebellion by Flemish citizens; instead they were soundly defeated,

Right: A padded cap for use under a helmet. Steel armour was very desirable booty, and after a battle the fallen were routinely stripped. A knight would often have encouraged his followers to help themselves to the simpler pieces, such as helmets, breastplates and arm defences, to add to their 'soft armour'.

Left: Gambesons for foot-soldiers are shown in period illustrations with sleeves extending down over the hands, and a high collar protecting the neck. The 'kettle-hat' helmet was ubiquitous throughout Europe, in various slightly differing forms.

and 700 French men-at-arms (including Count Robert) were killed. Due to the numbers of gilded spurs gathered up by the Flemish victors, this was popularly called the 'Battle of the Golden Spurs'. It was an early example of what a well-organized infantry force could achieve by exploiting familiar ground, thus preventing knights from unfolding their usually successful battle tactics. At Courtrai the rebels took up position in boggy terrain cut by many streams, into which the impatient French knights foolishly charged. Rural peasant-farmers found that they could achieve the same results as citizens; at the pass of Morgarten in 1315 a force of only 1,300 Schwyz foot-soldiers killed nearly 2,000 Austrian knights by clever use of their mountain terrain. Apart from picking their ground and tactics carefully, the most crucial key to effective infantry tactics was to instil in the peasantry and poorer citizens the belief that, armed with long pole-weapons, they could prevail against mounted men-at-arms if they held together stubbornly.

War gear

Of course, in terms of the quality and completeness of his equipment the typical infantry soldier of the 13th century was not comparable with even the poorest knight. Miniature paintings, such as those in the 'Maciejowski Bible' painted around 1250, suggest that the typical foot-soldier wore only a padded fabric gambeson as body armour, though this was probably made with several additional layers compared with those intended to be worn beneath ring-mail. Besides general appearance, the miniatures convey information about several details; they show the stiffness of this type of armour, and even how it was now fastened down the back by a row of buttons (the contemporary

Right: From his everyday costume a soldier of the lower social classes could not be distinguished from a farmer or an artisan, since all wore the same kinds of garments. Caped hoods were extremely practical, and were popular throughout Europe. Note the hanging purse.

Bottom of page: Fastening the hose to the belt of the braies with laces.

technique was to sew these to the actual edge of the garment, not off-set so that the buttonholes overlapped the edge).

Over the usual type of padded cap the infantryman wore a steel helmet. From the mid-13th century onwards this usually had a broad rim; resembling a cooking pot or a brimmed hat, this *chapel-de-fer* was referred to as a 'kettle-hat' or 'war hat', and gave relatively good protection against vertical cuts and falling arrows. Surviving examples show many detail differences – with the brims wide and flat, or narrower and down-turned, and with the crowns domed, flat-topped, conical or 'onion-shaped'.

Weapons

The primary weapons of most foot-soldiers were pole-arms, which could be used to hold an armoured man-at-arms on horseback beyond the range at which he could use his sword. In their most primitive form these had evolved from peasants' agricultural tools such as scythes and pitchforks, and they could be manufactured cheaply and in quantity by village blacksmiths. Beside the classical long spear, a wide range of other forms were seen in the 13th and 14th centuries. The most numerous were various local designs of the *halberd*, a shafted weapon with a heavy cutting blade furnished with a thrusting point at the end and often another, sometimes hooked, on the rear edge of the head. The halberd was suitable for both heavy, chopping blows and for stabbing thrusts, and the rear spike or hook could also be used for pulling horsemen out of the saddle. In their different guises these weapons (called 'bills' in England) became very common from the 13th century onwards. A secondary weapon was normally carried for close-up work and self defence – usually a large all-purpose knife, but occasionally a hatchet.

Costume

The civilian costume of a typical soldier in the 13th century was still very little changed from that of previous times. The main garment was a tunic or kirtle made from woollen cloth, worn over a linen shirt and braies and a pair of separate woollen hose. In cold weather a simple cloak was added, when available, but a useful compromise affordable by all classes was a generously cut caped hood covering the head and most of the shoulders (called in German a *Gugel)*. The woollen cloth used for making such hoods, and indeed all outdoor garments, was of a densely woven quality with a felted surface. As modern 'living history' re-enactors and experimental archaeologists can confirm, this made the cloth relatively windproof and to some degree water-repellent, keeping the wearer warm even when he was wet.

The costume was completed by the usual turn-shoes, and a leather belt for carrying the simple everyday necessities: a knife, and a pouch or 'purse'. In medieval times, when clothes were not furnished with pockets, such small bags were essential for carrying things like fire-strikers and tinder and, of course, money. This made them very attractive to a specialist class of thieves; like the 'pickpockets' who are descended from them, these were named after their profession – 'cut-purses'.

Crossbowman

Mid-13th Century

The bow and arrow have played a major role in history since prehistoric times, both as a hunting weapon and on the field of human conflict. The most striking evidence for this is probably 'Ötzi', the name given to the man whose body was found mummified in the ice high on the Hauslab-Joch in the Ötztaler Alps on the Austrian/Italian border. He died about 5,000 years ago – struck by an arrow whose flint head was found still lodged in a 2cm (0.8in) wide wound near his left shoulder blade.

A bow and arrows can be made with only a limited number of tools and relatively simple materials, and for thousands of years they offered the unique advantage of being able to strike a target over a longer distance than any thrown weapon. In some cultures, such as that of the horse-orientated nomadic peoples of the eastern and central Eurasian plains, the bow became the main armament. In the West, too, archaeological finds indicate that it was in common use throughout many centuries. For the purposes of this book we may note that the Bayeux Tapestry, illustrating the Norman invasion of England in 1066, shows archers with bows. (These should properly be termed 'self-' or 'simple' bows, since they had not yet achieved the size and power of the great 'war-bow' or 'longbow'.)

The military use of the bow in Europe reached its peak during the 14th and 15th centuries, when English/Welsh armies, in particular, fielded large numbers of archers with notable success. A huntsman with a bow can stalk his prey, and take careful aim to bring down a single target, but in the military context the best effect was achieved by concentrating numerous bowmen into a single group for mass effect. Due to their high rate of shooting – ten or even twelve arrows per minute – a force of several thousand archers shooting at a high angle was able to place a positive hailstorm of arrows into a defined area, effectively neutralizing advancing enemy troops long before they were able to get within range to use their own weapons.

'Mechanical' bows

Even during the ancient period, technicians had already started to develop devices able to mechanically store the energy necessary to propel a projectile, so that the shooter did not have to exert his bodily strength and was able to concentrate on recognizing and aiming at targets. Roman engineers successfully constructed several types of 'artillery' pieces that harnessed the torsion effect – the energy stored by twisting bundles of rope under

pressure – to project both stones and large arrows. Due to their size and relatively slow rate of 'fire' the use of these machines was mostly limited to fixed positions. Smaller crossbows using wooden staves were also known, but due to their relatively low power their use was generally limited to hunting; for battle, the Roman army had specialist archers with powerful composite bows. With the downfall of the Roman Empire torsion catapults fell out of use, but crossbows survived in the hunting field.

By the end of the first millennium AD the crossbow had been developed from a purely hunting weapon into a weapon of war. Increasingly, fragments of crossbows appear among the finds from archaeological excavations of manor sites dated to this period.

Right: A lightly equipped crossbowman takes aim during a practice session, wearing only his civilian costume of a woollen kirtle and hose, with the padded cap made to be worn beneath a ring-mail hood and/or a helmet (in his case, probably of 'war-hat' type). The shooting position, much like that with a modern firearm, made the crossbow a relatively easy weapon to master, and it required no great physical strength. Note the spanning-hook hanging from the front of his belt.

Above: Spanning his bow (here held upside down – note the trigger lever), he rests a foot in the stirrup and presses the weapon down towards the ground. The spanning-hook attached to his belt is engaged with the bowstring, and by straightening his leg and body he pulls the string back.

Above right: The bowstring is hooked over the upper projection of the nut, which is fixed by the internal trigger mechanism, and a bolt can now be loaded into the groove ahead of the nut. Note the composite bowstring.

By the 12th century at the latest, technical development had reached the point where the performance of the crossbow offered a challenge to that of an average self-bow. Much stronger versions appeared when the wooden stave cut from a single piece of a tree was replaced by a laminated stave, using several layered pieces of horn, wood and sinew grooved and glued together under pressure. The crossbow was now inflicting such serious wounds that, at the Second Lateran Council in 1139, the Church banned it as too frightful for use in conflicts between Christians (though its continued use against heathen enemies was explicitly allowed). The effect of this attempted 'arms

control' decree was quite limited, and the further development of the crossbow continued without interruption.

Increasing power and complexity

During the 14th century the technical limits for the use of wooden and composite bowstaves were reached, since no further increase in power was achievable. However, the techniques of steel production had by now improved to the point where high-quality steel was available in sufficient quantities – and at affordable prices – for crossbows to be fitted with a flat steel stave.

In parallel with the development of the bowstave, the methods of 'spanning' (bending the bowstave for loading) had also had to improve. While the early wooden types could be spanned by hand, the stronger wooden and composite bows required other means. The shooter's foot had to be placed in an iron stirrup at the front end of the stock; the shooter bent forward to engage the bowstring with a hook suspended from his belt, and then straightened his body. The first mention, dated to the year 1239, reports that the Emperor Frederick II ordered *balistas bonas de duobus pedibus* for his army.

Even this technique was practical only over a limited range of bowstave power, so more complex mechanical spanning devices had to be introduced for the increasingly powerful weapons, especially those with steel staves. These devices came in different designs: the 'goatsfoot lever' used simple leverage; the 'English winch' or 'German winch' used a winding-handle ratcheting a cogwheel along a toothed rail; and there were even machines employing two winding-handles, cords and pulley-wheels. The need for such elaborate means of spanning reduced the crossbows' rate of shooting significantly, and would more or less limit their use to fixed positions such as castle walls.

Tactics

The military use of crossbows is quite well documented. For example, Genoese crossbowmen were mentioned as early as 1012. According to several sources, Genoa seems long to have been a centre for the manufacture of high-quality weapons as well as for the 'export' of well-trained mercenary crossbowmen. In 1246 it was recorded that 500 Genoese took part in a campaign against Milan equipped with laminated crossbows; the Milanese casualties were so shocking that it was ordered that any crossbowman captured should have one hand cut off and one eye blinded. During a siege of Brest in 1388, crossbow 'snipers' made it fatally dangerous for the besieged defenders to lift their heads above the parapet of the city walls.

Crossbowmen were always fielded in formed units. By the end of the 12th century the French were already deploying their first crossbow companies, and such units, regarded as elite troops, normally fought in the front rank. Later it became routine for crossbowmen to deploy in teams of two; the second man erected a *pavise* shield with a prop, and from its shelter he could defend the shooter while he reloaded. The value of crossbowmen was such that it became worth the expense of mounting some of them for rapid deployment on campaign, and mounted crossbowmen often provided personal guards for important noblemen.

With the rising wealth and military needs of towns, their citizens also adopted this weapon; as early as 1286 the town of Schweidnitz held a crossbow-shooting competition, with a wooden bird as target. Crossbows were relatively expensive, and towns had to employ specialist craftsmen to make and maintain them; but they were easier to shoot from the shelter of battlements than conventional bows, and could be rested on parapets for a steady aim.

Above: The quiver usually contained twelve bolts, carried points upwards. The body of the quiver was made from thin wood covered with leather, parchment, or sometimes even with furry hide.

Below: The bolt is held below the head while it is placed in the groove on top of the stock, and its tail-end is pushed back into the top groove of the nut and against the string. For the sake of safety the bowman holds the weapon with his fingers between the stock and the trigger lever; knocking the trigger upwards would discharge the bow.

Above: The loaded crossbow. From this angle we can clearly see the fastenings of the stirrup and the bowstave, the thickness of the composite bowstring, and the design of the bolt.

the bowstave by means of multiple leather strips. These were doubtless wound around it while soaking wet, so that as they dried out they would shrink and tighten the binding.

The bowstave of this crossbow is still made from a single piece of yew wood. It rests in a deep cut-out at the nose of the stock, and is held in place by a massive binding made from a skein of rope and finally 'whipped' with cord; this passes through a hole bored through the sides of the stock further back. The bowstave is lacquered to protect it from humid air or rain, which would make it loose most of its power. This safeguard was even more vital for composite bows, since humidity could dissolve the glue holding the different elements of the stave together. Compared with the string of a contemporary longbow, the bowstring of a crossbow is notably thicker; it is made using many lengths of linen twine twisted together, and finally reinforced by a winding of linen yarn.

A groove is cut into the top of the stock at the forward end, into which the projectile or 'bolt' is laid. The single most vital element of the crossbow is positioned at the rear end of this groove – the 'nut', which holds the string back in the loaded position. Countersunk into the stock and mounted on a pivot like a wheel, it was normally made from antler, bone or metal. The nut was an irregular cylinder; it was cut with a perpendicular slot in a projection at the top for the end of the bolt, an intersecting axial slot in the rear for the string, and, hidden inside the hollowed stock, another 'step' on the underside of the nut that engaged the inner end of a pivoting metal trigger lever that passed up into the stock. When the bowman pulled the outer end of the trigger upwards against the bottom of the stock, the inside end disengaged from the nut; this revolved under the pressure of the string, and released it.

The bolts are of a short, compact design, and have only two simple horizontal 'flights' glued and tied into the grooved rear of the thick shaft. (Long, thinner shafts – like those of longbow arrows – oscillate due to the force transmitted by the string during the shot, resulting in an initially unstable flight.) Like arrowheads, the bolt heads could be of different shapes for different purposes; for example, a short, rhomboid head, as very commonly found in archaeological excavations, has good ballistic qualities for penetrating armour. The effective range (i.e., with a high probability of a hit) of late medieval crossbows fitted with composite or steel staves was much greater than that of a contemporary hand-gun. For example, the 'Dunstable Chronicles' report that in 1418/19 King Henry V of England got no closer to the besieged city of Rouen than '40 rods' or 'within a bolt shot' – a distance of approximately 200m (or yards).

The quiver in which the bolts are carried is made from wood covered with leather, and is slung from a waist belt. The bolts are carried with their points upwards, so it is shaped wider at the bottom to accommodate their flights; experience proved it was easier to load bolts if they were pulled out of the quiver head-first, while the opposite was true of longbow arrows. Finally, the crossbowman has a wider belt from which his spanning-hook is suspended. When on campaign he would certainly carry a secondary weapon for self-defence at close quarters, probably a short sword or a hatchet.

From the viewpoint of medieval military leaders, the crossbow's most important advantages over the longbow were that it required much less physical strength (so making it easier to recruit crossbowmen than longbowmen), and that it took much less time to train a man in its use. Once it was loaded it could be carried for as long as necessary, ready to shoot in an instant. Obviously, it took many hours of practice in regular sessions to achieve consistent accuracy with a crossbow, but not nearly as long as the years needed to master the longbow.

Weapon and equipment

Our reconstructed crossbowman may be imagined as attending a training session some time in the middle of the 13th century.

Looking at the crossbow itself, we see that the central element is the stock (or 'tiller'), which is carved from some hard wood. Starting at the 'business end' of the stock, we can see the iron foot-stirrup intended to ease the loading procedure, which is located in a slot cut in the nose of the stock, and attached to

Above: The bowman has pressed the trigger upwards, the nut has revolved, and the released string hurls the bolt through the air.

Below: This miniature from the *Chroniques de France ou de St Denis*, probably from the workshop of the so-called 'Virgil Master'. dates from some time after 1380. It depicts a battle for a bridge over the Seine during the Hundred Years' War. On the left bank, wearing dark blue 'soft armour', is a French crossbowman; on the crest of the bridge are two English longbowmen. Unlike the other foot-soldiers, who have leg armour, the crossbowman is protected only by a helmet, mail hood and gambeson – he needs to be agile and unencumbered.

regnmo procerum vel milicii
regni eadm in tempoze. bo

in tra ea quadruplex in eue
antea retio texta comista a
mundi gruoz opens r orribe
septemtrio Sit q eulibet prep
regni in eius regmine r a

The Longbowman

First Half of 14th Century

Although it was the English and Welsh archers in the armies of the Plantagenet kings who became the most renowned of medieval times, the 'longbow' (a later, not a medieval, term) was in fact recognized as a powerful weapon throughout continental Europe. Our reconstructed bowman might have been encountered in France, the Low Countries, the Holy Roman Empire, or elsewhere during the 14th century. All that we can tell from looking at him is that his equipment is of high quality, so he must be a professional soldier in the well-paid employment of a lord or a city. Unlike the crossbow or the gunpowder firearms that appeared later, the longbow demanded a physically strong man trained for many years (in the English tradition, from his seventh birthday onwards) in order to exploit its full potential. As a skilled specialist an archer could expect the wages of a craftsman, so only the wealthiest nobles or towns could afford to employ the large numbers of such men needed on the battlefield.

Trials with modern copies of medieval longbows have determined that they might have a draw-weight (the force needed to pull the string fully back) of up to 60kg (130lb). A well-practiced archer was able to loose ten to twelve arrows a minute out to a range of at least 200m (or yards), and could reach half again that distance at a slower rate, dropping every arrow within an area of a few square yards. Such power and skill could only be acquired by a strong young man learning his craft over perhaps ten years. Since permanent 'standing armies' were unknown in medieval times, suitable civilians had to practise constantly so as to remain fit to serve whenever their lord issued a summons to war, and in England laws were passed ensuring that yeomen trained 'at the butts' every Sunday in preference to any other sport.

The study of archers' skeletons recovered from the wreck of the Tudor warship *Mary Rose* reveals that their long and intense training influenced their physical development, specifically that of the left shoulder and arm, which show significant differences from those of other skeletons. The result of this physical investment was a superior battlefield effectiveness. Pulling the string of the heaviest bows back to the chin or ear before loosing gave the arrow a velocity of up to 45m (147ft) per second, enabling the penetration (though only at appropriate ranges and angles of strike) of all kinds of contemporary armour, both mail and plate. Tests have achieved the penetration of oak planks 2cm (0.8in) thick even at quite long range.

The military use of this formidable weapon ended in Europe only after the widespread introduction of hand-held firearms in the 16th century, although the bow has remained popular as a hunting and target weapon to this day. Its replacement was not due to firearms offering any superiority in battle. As was passionately argued by contemporaries, firearms of the 16th century could not approach the rate of shooting, or the accuracy at anything above the shortest range, of the longbow in the hands of a skilled archer (indeed, this remained the case well into the 19th century). The main reason for the change lay in that qualifying phrase 'a skilled archer'. To train a bowman up to his and his weapon's full potential took many years of frequently repeated practice, while a musketeer could be trained in a day or

Right: Our reconstructed bowman at the draw. The motion was described as 'shooting *in* a bow', and examination of identified skeletons of archers reveals deformation of the left shoulder and arm, which held the bow braced. The 'back' of his bowstave, facing us, shows the yellowish colour of the yew sapwood.

two to reach the (very limited) potential of his firearm. A second reason was the shortage of raw materials. Constant demand over several hundred years for high-quality timber from the yew tree – the best wood for making bows – had greatly reduced Europe's natural stock of these trees, with a consequent increase in price.

The weapon

The extraordinary capabilities of the longbow were a consequence of the composition, thickness and length of its limbs. The stave was cut and shaped from a single piece of yew, incorporating both the stretchable yellow 'sapwood' on the outside and the compressible reddish 'heartwood' on the inside. The finished bow was ideally between 1.7m (5ft 7in) and 1.9m (6ft 2in) long, and tapered down from a thickness of 2.85cm (1.12in) in the middle, with a flattened D-shaped cross-section. To achieve consistently accurate shooting the archer, his bow and his arrows all needed to be carefully matched. His height and arm-length determined the length of the stave and the maximum draw, and thus the arrow length (usually at least 81cm/ 32in).

Arrows were produced on an industrial scale; there was much variation, but the best shafts seem to have been made of aspen, and shaped slightly thicker towards the tail to withstand the powerful thrust of the string. They were supplied in 'sheaves' of twenty-four or thirty together, packed in barrels or cylindrical canvas sacks. To achieve a high shooting rate archers often stuck the arrows into the ground in front of them. Medieval arrowheads were made in different shapes designed for specific

Below: These 'personal' arrows are of higher quality than those provided in their hundreds of thousands for campaigning armies. The shafts are painted with a red oxide pigment mixed with a lacquer based on linseed oil, to protect them against humidity, and the heads are copied from originals found in the Harz region of Germany.

Above: The *chapel-de-fer* helmet and the padded cap are reconstructed after paintings from the mid-13th century 'Maciejowski Bible'. The broad helmet rim was intended to give at least some protection to the face and shoulders from downwards blows and falling arrows. This is an expensively ornate example.

uses. These ranged from blunt wooden heads for hunting small birds, through broad barbed heads for inflicting deep, bleeding wounds on large animals, to long pointed heads of a rectangular section to penetrate mail, and short pyramidal heads to pierce plate armour.

War gear

Like crossbowmen, archers were not intended to fight in battle at close quarters, though they naturally carried secondary weapons for self-defence. Our man's only steel protection is the 'kettle hat' or *chapel-de-fer,* with a riveted-in leather lining and worn over the usual padded linen *coif*. First popular during the 13th century, these helmets might be hammered down from single plates or assembled from separate riveted sections and bands, and some examples were quite elaborately shaped or decorated. In the later 14th and 15th century the iconography shows archers wearing various other types of helmet, with or without a ring-mail hood underneath. Popular examples seem to have been close-fitting cervellières, often shown with added *rondels* of plate covering the ears, and narrow-brimmed *sallets*. The ideal was to give protection without hampering the drawing of the bowstring to the face.

Our German archer – who may have to walk long distances when on campaign – prefers lightness and ease of movement to heavy armour, and his only body defence is a padded linen gambeson. Multiple layers of linen offered some protection against cuts; in this case (*see* pages 75 and 76) it is fastened with laces up the sides, to avoid a weak point at the front. It is made from natural, uncoloured fabric; some period illustrations show gambesons in various solid colours, or even 'parti-

Above: Close-quarter combat might sometimes be unavoidable, so a small 'buckler' shield might be carried in conjunction with a sword. This example is based on an original found in the Netherlands and now in an Amsterdam museum. It is made of poplar wood, with an iron boss and a brass rim, and covered with painted leather.

Left: The archer holds his bow with an arrow nocked to the string, ready to bring it up to the aim. The wide fabric sling over the shoulder supports a 'bread bag' at the archer's hip.

coloured', showing two contrasting colours divided laterally down the centre of the front and back. Paintings from 15th-century manuscripts, and a famous Flemish tapestry, show longbowmen with more substantial protection including short-sleeved mail shirts, *brigandines* (fabric vests with many small metal scales riveted between the inner and outer layers), or even steel breastplates. However, they never seem to wear leg armour.

The dagger was coming into widespread use during the 14th century, and, as the only weapon worn with civilian costume by professional warriors or people of higher social rank, it became an object of fashion. (Persons of lower status also wore sidearms, but these were still more universal tools than weapons.) The styling and decoration of hilt and sheath provided an opportunity for the owner to display his wealth – always an important consideration in the High Middle Ages – and our archer's dagger (*see* below) identifies him as a follower of the latest style. This type is what has been christened by English-speaking historians as a 'ballock dagger', in which the double swelling of the guard at the base of the handle consciously imitates the shape of the male genitals.

This particular piece, furnished with brass at the pommel and guard, is of above-average quality; simpler specimens had the complete hilt made from a single piece of wood.

The bowman's belt has metal 'stiffener' decorations; it carries his small table-knife (*see* below, in the light-brown sheath left of the hanging end of his belt), and a large pouch.

Apart from its main compartment containing items of daily use, the latter has two small additional drawstring bags sewn to the front. Typically these might contain some small coins to give to poor beggars as an act of Christian charity (men of war had reason to fear for the salvation of their immortal souls, and such donations might earn them a measure of divine mercy).

Finally, slung around his body is an early example of a soldier's canvas haversack or bread-bag. The logistics of medieval armies were not as primitive as is sometimes believed, and whenever it was practically possible the best commanders tried to ensure that their troops were issued basic rations. Especially during long marches, such provisions were essential to health and morale.

Costume

The bowman's clothing is, as usual, made from woollen fabric with good insulating characteristics, especially when wet. His most noticeable garment is his *Gugel* or deeply caped hood, here decorated with braid at the edges. An almost universal item of clothing during the High Middle Ages, it could be worn as a hood, or folded down around the neck as a thick scarf, or – when taken off and rolled up in a specific way – worn as a hat. As fashions changed over time the 'tail' or *liripipe* trailing from its apex grew increasingly longer. This could be wrapped around the neck over the hood as an additional muffler, and when it hung down the back it was tucked into the belt to control it.

Left: Our archer, seen here cleaning his nails with his 'ballock dagger', displays on his simple woollen cap a cast-tin badge showing that he has taken an opportunity to make a pilgrimage, for the good of his soul, to a French sanctuary dedicated to the Blessed Virgin Mary.

Below: During military campaigns archers were usually deployed together in great numbers, to achieve the maximum 'weapons effect'. English armies with at least 5,000 archers were not unusual; such a force could loose 50,000 shafts every minute at an enemy battle line.

Gador

howe worthy, debyded his battyls vpon A
Arge playne within the Cite. and howe he
ant the, doftretly to be vnder þe ledynge of
his brethere. and other worthy kynges

Then Amora with
hir pale

Officer and Foot-Soldier, 1485

The classic High Medieval era is judged by some historians to have ended in 1347, with the outbreak in Europe of the 'Black Death'. This virulent and almost invariably fatal plague coincided with several years of bad summer weather, ruined harvests and consequent famine, and together these disasters killed approximately 25 million people during only a few years. Europe lost almost one-third of its population; in some places, such as crowded trading cities, up to 80 per cent of the inhabitants died, and throughout the continent economic activity virtually ceased for a while.

During the 14th century the reduction in the relative military dominance of the mounted, armoured knight gradually continued, while the role of foot-soldiers steadily increased – a process accelerated by the use both of missile weapons and of disciplined mass formations equipped with pole-arms. Milestones in this continuous development were the English victories at Crécy (1346) and Poitiers (1356), when the armies of King Edward III and his son the Black Prince – both with large contingents of longbowmen – defeated stronger French armies and inflicted very high casualties. As the Hundred Years' War between England and France dragged on, the last significant English victory was won by King Henry V – again, largely thanks to his massed archers – at Agincourt in 1415. Like Courtrai in 1302, all these were essentially defensive victories; they were won by assembling thousands of bowmen on the flanks of bodies of men-at-arms dismounted to fight on foot, while a minority remained mounted to await the need or the opportunity to charge.

As it turned out, a still more significant episode was the siege and capture of Tannenberg castle in Hesse in the year 1399. The garrison's lengthy defence was aided by the use of crude hand-guns, but their besiegers had several heavy, wall-smashing gunpowder 'bombards', and the end came when a shot from one of these exploded the gunpowder store in the castle keep. During the 15th century the development and spread of heavy artillery would negate the centuries-old advantage of stone castles, but it was not until the turn of the 15th/16th centuries that hand-guns would become really significant on the open battlefield. Their potential for massed use at short range, filling the same tactical role as crossbows in supporting blocks of massed pikemen, would be developed by the Spanish general Gonzalo de Cordoba during campaigns in Italy in 1495–1503. (However, while these mixed infantry tactics would go on to dominate the warfare of the Renaissance period, cavalry protected by at least partial armour would retain a role for another 150 years.)

Simultaneously with these 15th-century military developments came other events and innovations that would shape European history significantly. In 1453 the westwards and northwards spread of the Ottoman Turkish empire in the Middle East was capped by Sultan Mehmet II's final capture of Constantinople, capital of the Byzantine Empire. This would bring Muslim and Christian face to face once again throughout the Mediterranean world. At the same time, the perfection in Germany of the method of printing texts with movable type (popularly ascribed to Johann Gutenberg of Mainz) would soon allow the widespread production of books at prices affordable by the nobility, at least. Among many social consequences of this world-changing achievement, the study of military texts from the Classical world would advance the sophistication of military tactics.

Right: For combat on foot our reconstructed officer wears a suit of complete plate with a ridged, fluted finish in the German style. Note the hammerhead projection on the rear of the head of his pole-axe.

The suit of complete plate

In Britain the end of the Middle Ages is generally dated to 1485, when the victory of the future King Henry VII over King Richard III at Bosworth Field brought the long and very destructive internal 'Wars of the Roses' to a close. The second half of the 15th century saw the most distinctive part of knightly equipment – the suit of plate armour – reach its peak of technical development. It is sometimes imagined that such equipment was so heavy and constricting that a knight who fell over was helpless, but this is a misconception; it is based on surviving examples of very heavy and inflexible tournament armours, made specifically for charging single opponents in a straight line. Obviously, when a knight went into combat his life depended not just on complete protection but also on being able to move and use his weapons freely, and late-15th century battle armours were masterpieces of technical craftsmanship.

Above: The combination of the sallet and the bevor give good overall protection for the head and neck. The only handicap is the very limited field of vision through the shallow frontal slit.

Previous centuries had seen full ring-mail armour gradually reinforced with additional plate defences, and by the end of the 14th century these had merged to form a complete, connected suit of plate. Ring-mail was now only used beneath it to protect the areas where rigid plates could not be attached, such as the armpits and groin. The man-at-arms reconstructed on pages 81– 85 wears a typical 'white' (i.e. polished) armour of German style, and its superior quality suggests that he holds high rank within some professional military organization. We might term him an 'officer', though not necessarily a knight; during the late Middle Ages professional fighting men of more humble birth acquired more importance, and the talented could rise to hold medium or even senior commands. Plagues and generations of warfare had taken a serious toll of the knighthood and military nobility, opening opportunities for their social inferiors, and since these men were paid well they could often afford equipment of high quality. (The armour of noblemen might also be acquired as the booty of war, of

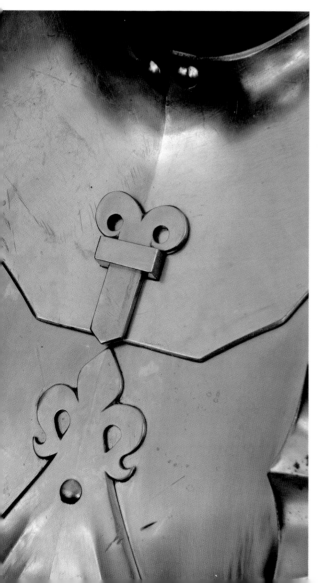

Left: The bevor is fixed to the breastplate by a decorated wedge through a bracket projecting through a slot in the bevor. The additional reinforcing plate over the lower part of the breastplate, here drawn up into a *fleur-de-lys* shape, is termed a *plackart*.

Right: During the 14th-century development of plate armour for the arms the elbow was at first protected by a disc over the outer surface of the joint. This turned out to be less than effective, and in time it was replaced by a complex 'wrap-around' couter, with a large projection to throw off the blows of opponents' weapons. The separate elements of the arm protection are articulated by means of rivets in slots that allow them to slide over one another as the limb flexes and stretches. The deep cuff-plate of the gauntlet and the couter almost meet over the *vâmbrace* forearm plates.

Above: With his helmet removed, our sweating officer has lowered the upper plate of the bevor over the lower plate, revealing the interior padding. This was necessary, since a blow on the bevor would otherwise drive it forcefully against the mouth and chin. The rondel protecting the vulnerable armpit is also clearly visible; hung on a strap, it does not limit the movement of the arm. Note, too, the pyramidal projections on the knuckles of the gauntlet; these give stability, throw off blows, and are useful for delivering them in hand-to-hand combat. The halberd-like head of the heavy pole-axe is secured to both sides of the squared wooden shaft with nailed iron *langets*, to prevent it being chopped off in combat.

course, but the best plate armours had to be articulated so exactly that they were made to measure for individuals.)

Although these armours were intended to be used on horseback, from the mid-14th century it was quite common for heavily armoured men-at-arms to fight on foot – as often by choice, for reasons of terrain and tactics, as because they had been unhorsed. The best armours were provided as a complete 'kit' with alternative elements, and for use on foot some parts would temporarily be replaced. For example, the heavy shoulder-guards (*pauldrons*) were replaced, as on our reconstructed officer, with lighter hanging *rondels* to protect the armpits.

However, the articulated plates below the waist (*faulds*), and those on the front of the thighs (*tassets),* are both retained here. Designed for use when riding, they also give enough

flexibility for a man fighting on foot; the separate plates are mounted overlapping on internal straps, loosely enough to allow the necessary range of movement.

Late 15th-century armours gave both a high degree of protection and surprising mobility, although they did nothing to ease the age-old problem of ventilation and the threat of heatstroke. The 'fluting' on several pieces of this armour is not only a matter of German fashion; it gave additional stability, allowing the use of thinner and lighter plate, and was also meant to prevent the points of enemy weapons sliding off into a vulnerable gap.

The man-at-arms had to find an optimal balance between protection and mobility. In our officer's case, complete mail sleeves and leggings filling in all gaps in the suit of plate would have considerably increased the armour's overall weight. Under his armour he has chosen to wear only his strong linen 'arming doublet', reinforced with leather strips and lightly padded where the plates chafe. Cord laces sewn to the doublet at various places (e.g. the shoulders) pass through holes in some plates and are knotted to attach them. Such doublets sometimes had sections of mail sewn directly to them in the vulnerable areas, and were coupled with special 'arming hose' made of strong whipcord, with either attachment laces or holes for armour-straps.

Limb armour

The separate parts of the arm protection are fixed together with mushroom-headed rivets that engage with long slots, thus allowing the plates to slide back and forth over one another. At the elbow a large *couter* of complex shape protects both the outside and inside of the joint. The same rivet-and-slot principle is used in the manufacture of the armoured gloves (*gauntlets*); on the basis of a leather glove, articulated plates cover the wrist, the back of the hand and the parts of each finger.

The complete leg armour has a slim fit following the natural shape of the leg, very like the slim-fitting civilian hose of that period. The shin of the greaves has a raised keel, giving extra strength against frontal impacts. The *poleyn* protects the knee even when it is bent, with a 'wing' at the outside to stop cuts at the inside of the joint. The poleyns are adjustable in height by alternative holes engaging locator pins, to allow the armour to be worn by different persons without having to be altered by a specialist armourer.

Head and neck protection

The elegantly shaped *sallet* helmet, with its vision slit, slightly flared rim, and long, pointed neck-guard, does not originally belong with the suit of armour our officer is wearing. It was modelled on an original helmet made in around 1485 by a

master-armourer in the town of Landshut and kept today in the armouries at Schwäbisch-Gmünd, east of Stuttgart in southern Germany. The line of rivets all around the skull secures the internal liner in place.

Below the rim of the sallet the throat and lower part of the face are protected by a *bevor*. In this case its rigid attachment to the breastplate is evidence that it was designed for use by a mounted man-at-arms, who would have preferred additional protection against the lance of an opponent rather than mobility for his head. A spring-loaded stud connects the overlapping upper and lower plates of the bevor; when this is pressed it allows the upper plate to be lowered – for instance, so that the wearer could have a drink, or simply breathe more freely during a pause in his exhausting activity, without taking the whole bevor off.

By now the almost universal use of full plate armour has rendered the use of a shield redundant. For foot combat our officer has both hands free to wield a pole-axe; with a shaft about 1.25m (4ft) long, this has an axe-blade and spearhead like a halberd, but with a war-hammer instead of a spike on the rear of the head. It is thus a deadly cutting, stabbing and crushing weapon even against an armoured opponent. His secondary weapon, and a sign of his profession, is a long dagger.

Right: The leg armour, including the poleyn protecting the knee, is manu-factured along the same principles as that for the arm. Note the locator pin and holes that allow the poleyn to be fitted to the greaves for different lengths of leg. For combat on foot the shoes are hobnailed for extra grip; even though the armour allows remarkable freedom of movement, to slip and fall over while in close combat might easily be fatal.

THE FOOT-SOLDIER

This reconstruction shows a typical representative of the foot-soldiers equipped with pole-arms who formed the bulk of most late 15th-century armies – except in England, where archers still outnumbered what were called 'bill-men' (from the English term for a halberd or similar weapon).

By this date the infantry were often well protected with plate armour, though not in complete suits like the men-at-arms; they might sometimes lack leg armour. Armies usually formed up for battle in three 'divisions': a vanguard, a main body, and a reserve. Within each division, blocks of these heavy infantry together with dismounted men-at-arms provided the central mass, with cavalry on the flanks or held back in the main reserve. In continental European armies the missile troops – archers, crossbowmen and perhaps hand-gunners – usually deployed

Below: In the melée of infantry combat the halberdier has knocked over a man-at-arms, and now seeks to finish him off with a stab through his unarmoured armpit.

forwards between the pole-arm blocks. They would open the battle by trying to weaken and disorder the enemy formations in preparation for an attack by heavy infantry or cavalry, or to goad them into attacking while at a disadvantage.

The effective range of arrows and bolts was 200–250m/yd, and of bullets perhaps half that. Under the lash of these missiles, opposing troops would have an incentive to move forward and close with the enemy in order to get out of this 'killing zone'. One side might actually break and fall back before close contact was made, but when armies did come together the fighting was savage. Each man in the first rank or two hacked and stabbed at those who faced him, and when men fell those behind them stepped forward to take their place. If a gap was forced in one

Top of page: This very broad-brimmed *chapel-de-fer* incorporates a vision slit in the base of the front brim.

Right: At the base of the backplate, the movable faulds are attached by means of rivets sliding in slots. Even cheaper 'ammunition' armour purchased in quantity and issued by employers was of reasonable quality, though it might not fit perfectly.

Below: The shoulder, where the breast- and backplates buckle together over the mail cape. Note the top arm plate laced to the gambeson beneath it, by means of metal-tipped cords called 'points'.

block of troops, and exploited aggressively, then that whole formation might unravel quickly as men lost confidence. Then their victors could turn to take another block in the flank, and the whole army might break and flee. Sometimes the winners were too exhausted to pursue, but if they did then the losers would be butchered without mercy – apart from the noblemen, whose capture and ransoming brought rich rewards to their captors.

Our halberdier wears a very deep, wide-brimmed 'kettle hat' that protects part of his shoulders as well as his head, and has a slit in the base of the front brim that gives him minimal

forward vision if he bends his head. This design would be useful in siege warfare, as it protects him from missiles or stones from the walls above him. Under it he wears a caped ring-mail collar or 'standard', fixed to the high collar of his padded gambeson.

Over the gambeson his body and arms are protected by plate defences made in the German style, though the torso and arm plates do not fit together well, leaving vulnerable gaps. This armour was probably issued as separate pieces from the arsenal

Left: Details of the dagger, pouch, couter, vâmbrace, and Italian gauntlet. Visible here hanging down from underneath the gambeson are the metal-tipped ends of the 'points' that lace together the soldier's woollen doublet and single-piece hose. The latter also have a small laced flap at the crotch, for the same purpose as the fly of modern trousers.

of his employer. (The great majority of the 'suits' of armour seen today in museums and other collections are composite, i.e. assembled from separate components rather than originally made as an integrated set by a single armourer's workshop.)

The type of gauntlet that our soldier is wearing, characterized by just a few large, smooth plates over the back of the hand and upper fingers, was first manufactured by Italian armourers but came into widespread use throughout Europe. It was cheaper to produce than the fingered types made in Germany, so was favoured by the less wealthy and by employers procuring armour in quantity.

The different elements of armour, both 'soft' and 'hard', could be worn in different combinations. Brigandines were very common in this period, and even full ring-mail shirts might still be worn. While a gambeson could not stop the thrust of a bladed weapon or the direct hit of an arrow or bolt at short range, it gave good protection against deflected blows or even missiles that had lost much of their energy.

Our foot-soldier's secondary weapon is a long dagger, worn from his belt and held steady behind his pouch. The type illustrated is called today a 'rondel dagger', from the circular shape of the pommel and guard. The dagger was now a standard sidearm for close combat, with a long, pointed blade for thrusting through visor slots, between the joints of plate armour, or to burst through ring-mail. The belt illustrated here has a punched pattern, and its decorative brass fittings show its high quality.

Above: The high-quality dagger blade is made using the 'damascene' technique, by which rods of mild, flexible steel and harder steel are forged together to form a composite material that is both flexible and sharp. Many of even the everyday medieval knives that have been found were made by this method. Especially from the 16th century onwards, the pattern of the welded rods was made visible by etching to produce a decorative effect.

Left: The decoration of the belt. Note also that the gambeson is in this case laced together at the front.

Costume

Beneath his armour the 15th-century soldier still wore a very long, loose linen shirt and linen braies, though the latter were now shorter than previously and more like modern underpants. The woollen hose had integral feet, and were closely cut in a single piece like a modern pair of 'tights' rather than with separate legs. They were no longer suspended from the waist-cord of the braies, but were attached around the waist of a short, close-fitting woollen jacket – the 'doublet' – by means of perhaps six sets of laces ('points') with metal tips. Fashionable doublets had a loose, puffed shape at the shoulders, though the arms and torso were closely tailored.

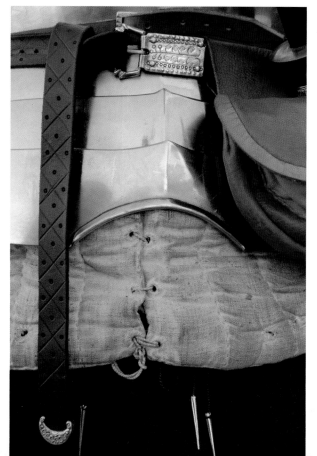

les hebrieux a
prez et oublierent
nostre seigne?
et se prindrent
a mal faire. si comme iz auoy
ent accoustume quant iz ne
auoyent point de prince. Dot
vindrent les madianiens
et les amalechiens et les a
rabiens. Et leur coururent
sus a grant puissance. Cex
qui eschapperent fuirent aux

montaignes et se muchoret
es fosses et la ou ilz pouoyent
mieulx. En telle doule? fu
rent les filz dysrael vng ane.
Apres ce nostre seigne?
eut merry deulz quant il vit
leur repentance. et mist ou
ceur de gedeon qui estoit de
la lignie manasse et filz ja
ab. sy estant hardiement. il
entreprint les filz dysrael
a deffendre. En ce temps les

The Armed Citizen, 1470–1500

Those who lived in cities fell into two categories. In German these might be termed *Inwohnern* or 'inhabitants', who lived within the walls but did not enjoy full civic rights, and the *Bürger* or 'citizens', who had such rights, but also the responsibility of defending their community when it faced attack.

Cities did not easily secure their status of semi-independence from the nobles or Church dignitaries who ruled their regions, and these quarrels often led to episodes of actual warfare. While sometimes bloody, such conflicts were usually brief, and concluded without too much destruction. After all, it was in nobody's interests to burn down a trading city or kill its population, since it was its continuing commercial success that made it a desirable possession in the first place. Coastal cities sometimes faced more menacing threats from foreign attackers, but from the mid-14th century many German cities on the North Sea and Baltic coasts and inland on the great navigable rivers formed a confederacy for mutual support. This Hanseatic League was a considerable naval power, though its citizen land forces had to be reinforced with mercenaries from elsewhere in Germany. Later such troops increasingly took over guard duties from the citizen militias even in peacetime.

By late medieval times most cities had armouries with stocks of military equipment to arm their citizens at times of need. These contained hand weapons and crossbows, protective armour of all kinds and, in the richest cities, firearms and artillery pieces. Beside items purchased by the municipal council these stores included items donated by wealthy citizens, or even gear that had been captured during conflicts. As evidenced by the 200-year-old lamellar armours excavated at Visby, such items might remain on the inventory of town armouries for generations on end. The armouries might be located in the city's council hall or, if space was not available there, in other functional buildings. Most public buildings served different purposes, and the attic floors were often used as granaries – therefore the citizens of Cologne, for example, called their armoury the 'Corn House'.

The stocks held in these armouries were administered by representatives of the city council. We are in debt to these city employees for valuable insights into the inventories of several armouries, since they produced numerous dated lists showing the exact numbers of arms and equipment in their care. The oldest known inventory lists the contents of the armoury of Basle in Switzerland, which was built in 1414. According to this list it held 324 crossbows with 6,000 bolts, sixty-eight hand-guns and seventeen artillery pieces. In the city of Dresden three armouries existed at the same time, and in 1409 the municipal armoury was installed in the city hall. Complete sets of armour were not usually issued to individual citizens, and the items handed out depended upon the duties to be fulfilled.

Right: Here our reconstructed guard at a city gate has taken off his helmet and wears his caped hood against cold weather; note that it is divided at the front, and fastens with buttons. The gambeson shows the puffed shape at the shoulders and upper sleeves that was then fashionable for civilian doublets and coats.

German city guard

This citizen is equipped with a gambeson, breast- and backplates, and leg armour. His weapon, known in German-speaking regions as a *Knebel-Spieß*, has a head similar that of the 'winged' spears used since early medieval times both for big-game hunting and for war (and often referred to simply as a 'boar spear').

The plate armour is of an exact fit, as can be seen in the close-up photos of the legs on page 92. The greaves protecting the shins follow the outline of his legs closely, and there is even a protrusion hammered into the steel to accommodate the anklebone. The front and rear sections of the greaves might be fastened together either by leather straps or, as in this case, by hinges on one side and, on the other, by studs engaging with holes in the overlapping edges and held in place by the tension of the close fit. The superior craftsmanship and precision of contemporary armourers (in Germany, clustered around southern centres such as Augsburg and Nuremberg) meant that even a full suit of armour did not restrict mobility. Many of the junctions between separate plates were fashioned with rivets

passing through slots in overlapping edges, which allowed the plates to slide back and forth as the wearer flexed his body without opening vulnerable gaps between them.

Just one example of the armourer's skill is seen at the knees. At the junction of the poleyns with the greaves below them, locator pins could be put through any of three different holes depending upon the wearer's leg length, so that the armour could be adjusted easily to fit men of different heights. The big, heart-shaped 'wing' at the outside of the poleyn protects the hollow of the knee joint from cuts from the side.

On page 93, our city guard has laid aside his *Gugel* and put on a strapped bevor and a deep sallet of a type seen all over Central Europe. Unlike that worn by the reconstructed officer on pages 81–83, this helmet has a large separate visor over the face. This can be raised by swivelling it upwards on two rivets through its upper corners, and locks down in place by means of a spring-loaded catch through the lower right corner. The shallow vision slit across the visor has raised lips to prevent an enemy's blade sliding inside as it glances over the surface of the polished steel. Again, the helmet-wearer's vision is poor; he can see clearly enough straight ahead, but the peripheral vision is restricted and, most dangerously, he cannot see anyone who gets close to him below his line of sight. The raised 'keel' that has been hammered into the skull and visor during construction has the effect of strengthening the steel along an axis that was always vulnerable to blows.

To the medieval mind, any opportunity to decorate a functional object should be taken, and the rather sinister elegance of this helmet is interrupted by a double row of large, fluted knobs running round the lower sides of the skull. These are the extended ends of rivets which secure a substantial liner of padded fabric inside the helmet, as well as chin straps from four attachment points to hold it securely in place.

Opposite page: Details of the finely fitted leg armour, which is attached to a sleeveless black arming vest by 'points' and supported by leather straps to a belt, as well as by red straps buckled around the thighs, knees and calves. The poleyns, of typical German shape, are articulated by rivets sliding in slots to allow flexing, and their attachment to the leg plates can be adjusted for height. The small plates at the top of the cuisses are articulated in the same way, and just below them a raised stop-rib prevents an enemy's blade from sliding up into the groin. Only foot-armour is needed to complete the total protection of the lower limbs. Ring-mail might be used for this, or complete 'iron shoes' made of finely articulated plates to allow the instep and toes to flex.

This page: The visored 'Burgundian' sallet, with its relatively short neck-guard. To unfasten the visor the wearer presses a spring-loaded stud at its lower right corner (*see* photo at bottom right). When the visor is lifted fully, pivoting on the two decorated rivets through its extended top corners, friction holds it up. The sources mention several occasions when knights in battle became so frustrated by their limited vision that they raised the visor, with fatal consequences. The fluted rivets secure both the thickly padded liner and the Y-shaped chin straps (*see* photo below). The inner surface shows a blackened anti-rusting finish.

The bevor is shaped in compound curves from a single plate; the squared slot low on its right is for a fastening bracket from a breastplate to pass through, but here the bevor and breastplate are two separate items from an armoury, not matched together. Most foot-soldiers (and indeed, many men-at-arms) must have worn such 'composite' armours.

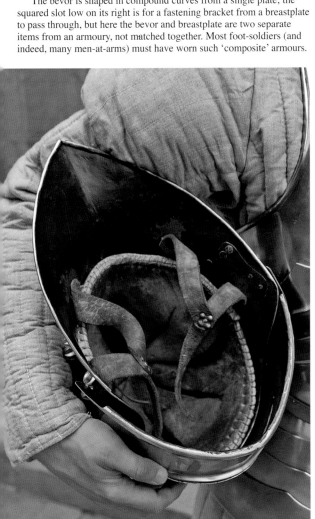

Left: Again, two rows of rivet heads around the skull of the barbute show the internal fixing of a padded liner and chin straps.

Right: For walking through the streets this citizen wears a hat, coif, short hooded cloak, and pattens under his shoes.

except for a helmet to protect his head from training accidents. This type of helmet was termed the *barbute* or *barbuta,* and was typical of 15th-century Italy, although – like Italian armour of all kinds – it was also widely seen in more northerly and western regions. (Italian armourers in such centres as Milan coupled effective methods of production with business sense and, since Italy was the cradle of sophisticated international banking, Italian traders spread their wares throughout the continent.)

The design of the barbute was clearly inspired by that of the ancient Classical type we nowadays call a 'Corinthian' helmet, and it offered a good compromise between protection and ease of vision and breathing. The painting of helmets was not purely decorative, but protected them against the ever-present danger of rusting. It was also fashionable among the wealthy to have barbutes covered with a glued-on layer of coloured velvet or other costly cloth.

The design of the sword's hilt and guard shows one of the typical variants seen during this period, while the pommel is characteristic of southern Germany. The blade had two 'fullers' or grooves running down it to reduce the weight of the weapon. Several 15th-century instruction manuals, such as that by Hans Talhoffer, illustrate in 'strip cartoon' format sophisticated methods of fencing with the long sword: grasping hilt and blade with one hand or both; using the edge, the point and the clubbed pommel; twisting, ducking and tripping, to unbalance or disarm an opponent and open the way for delivering the fatal blow.

Militiaman at training

From his clothing and gear, we might guess that this militiaman comes from a city in the southern Tyrol region bordering Italy, but there was so much trade interaction across Europe that few really specific local fashions can be identified from the sources. Like many of his fellow citizens, this member of a town militia has decided to take instruction in the art of fencing with the sword.

In earlier times the formal duel between two men had a purely judicial character; if one was accused of an offence, without witnesses, then the matter was put to the test of a duel, in the belief that God would give victory to the one who was telling the truth. Such personal confrontations became formalized when it became acceptable for these trials to be fought, according to fixed rules, by professional champions instead of by the actual parties to the case.

During the final part of the medieval era a growing number of fencing schools for citizens (so-called *scolae dimicantum*) operated in urban centres. The sword was the symbol of superior social status, and fighting with swords evolved into a respected 'craft'. As in the case of trade crafts, guilds were formed to administer the practice, and were responsible for granting titles such as 'fencing master'or 'journeyman fencer' after overseeing the appropriate tests. Under the instruction of these fencing-masters many citizens trained in the handling of different types of weapon, though over time the sporting, rather than the military character of the exercise became increasingly important.

On these pages our citizen prepares to train with the 'long sword'. In accordance with the rules of unarmoured fencing – so-called *Bloßfechten* – he is wearing only his civilian clothing

Costume

In chilly winter sunshine, our *Bürger* wears over his doublet and hose a thigh-length dark red 'coat' buttoned down the front, loosely cut in the upper sleeves but tight on the forearms. His slim-cut, one-piece hose are parti-coloured *(mi-parti* was the French term), with legs in different colours. To walk to and from the training ground, his leather shoes are protected from the muddy puddles and filth of medieval streets by wooden *pattens* strapped under the soles. He wears a linen coif under his woollen hat, both to keep his hair clean and to prevent the hat getting greasy. Over it all, he puts on a short cloak made of a thick, loden-style felted wool fabric, with a hood buttoned to it at the shoulders.

Modern re-enactors who have mastered these techniques for displays give an impression of brutal, lightning-fast athleticism.

As well as the long two-handed sword another, less elegant type was more suited to close combat in confined conditions, such as between closely formed infantry blocks. This was the *falchion* (called a *Malchus* in German-speaking regions), illustrated at top right of this page. This was a short, single-edged cutting weapon, with a scimitar-like blade that widened considerably towards the point. On the one hand, this extra mass gave it a powerful, chopping blow with a great deal of kinetic energy; on the other hand, the point-heavy shape made it unbalanced and quite difficult to handle with any dexterity. To make training with this weapon less dangerous the trainees often used weighted wooden replicas called *Dussacks*.

Left: The long hilt of this type of sword gave a two-handed grip, and perfect balance for complex fencing manoeuvres. Reversing the sword to crack an opponent's skull with the heavy pommel was a recognized move.

Top right: The cutlass-like falchion, an effective close-quarter weapon often used in conjunction with a small buckler or 'fist shield'. When strong drink had been taken, hot-blooded young men who habitually carried swords and bucklers frequently got into fights in the city streets.

Right: Here the steel buckler is hooked to a 'bread bag' for ease of carriage. This man wears no belt pouch, so such a bag is convenient for even a short journey.

Bibliography

Arbman, Holder, *Birka I Die Gräber – Untersuchungen und Studien.* (Vitterhets Historie och Antikvitets Akademien, 1943)

Boeheim, Wendelin, *Handbuch der Waffenkunde* [1890] (Akademische Druck- u. Verlagsanstalt, 1966)

Clark, John, *The Medieval Horse and its Equipment*, 2nd edition (Boydell & Brewer, 2004)

Cowgill, J., de Neergaard, M. and Griffiths, N., *Knives and Scabbards*, 2nd edition (Boydell & Brewer, 2000)

Crowfoot, Elisabeth, Pritchard, Frances and Staniland, Kay *Textiles and Clothing* 9th edition (Boydell & Brewer, 2012)

Egan, Geoff, *The Medieval Household* 3rd edition (Boydell & Brewer, 2012)

Egan, Geoff and Pritchard, Frances, *Dress Accessories* 4th edition (Boydell & Brewer, 2010)

Embleton, Gerry, *Europa Militaria Special No.8: Medieval Military Costume* (Crowood, 2000)

Geibig, Alfred, *Beiträge zur morphologischen Entwicklung des Schwertes im Mittelalter* (Wachholtz, 1991)

Goetz, Dorothea, *Die Anfänge der Artillerie* (Militärverlag, 1985)

Goubitz, Olaf, *Stepping through Time. Archaeological Footwear from Prehistoric Times until 1800*, 2nd edition (Spa, 2011)

Grape, Wolfgang, *The Bayeaux Tapestry* (Prestel, 1994)

Grew, Francis and de Neergaard, Margarethe, *Shoes and Pattens*, 8th edition (Boydell & Brewer, 2011)

Harmuth, Egon, *Die Armbrust* (Akademische Druck- und Verlagsanstalt, 1975)

Hist. Mus. der Pfalz Speyer (Hg.), *Die Wikinger. München* (Minerva, 2008)

Kohlmorgen, Jan, *Der mittelalterliche Reiterschild. Historische Entwicklung von 975 bis 1350* (Karfunkel, 2002)

Kühnel, Harry, *Bildwörterbuch der Kleidung und Rüstung* (Kröner, 1992)

Lehnart, Ulrich, *Kleidung & Waffen der Früh- und Hochgotik 1150–1320* (Karfunkel, 1998)

Lehnart, Ulrich, *Kleidung & Waffen der Spätgotik I 1320–1370* (Karfunkel, 2000)

Lehnart, Ulrich, *Kleidung & Waffen der Spätgotik II 1370–1420* (Karfunkel, 2003)

Lehnart, Ulrich, *Kleidung & Waffen der Spätgotik III 1420–1480* (Karfunkel, 2005)

LWL-Museum für Archäologie- Westf. Landesmuseum Herne, Aufruhr 1225, *Das Mittelalter an Rhein und Ruhr* (Zabern, 201

Mac Gregor, Arthur, *Bone, Antler, Ivory & Horn. The Technology of Skeletal Materials since the Roman Period* (Croom Helm, 1985)

Menghin, Winfried (Hg.), *Wikinger, Waräger, Normannen. Die Skandinavier und Europa 800–1200* (SMPK, 1992)

Müller, Heinrich, *Albrecht Dürer. Waffen und Rüstungen* (Zabern, 2002)

Müller-Boysen, Carsten, *Kaufmannsschutz und Handelsrecht im frühmittelalterlichen Nordeuropa* (Wachholtz, 1990)

Nørgård Jørgensen, Anne, *Waffen und Gräber. Typologische und chronologische Studien zu skandinavischen Waffengräbern 520/30 bis 900* (Nordiske Fortidsminder Serie B Vol. 17) (Koniglige Nordiske Oldskriftselskab, 1999)

Nurmann, Britta, Schulze, Carl and Verhülsdonk, Torsten, *Europa Militaria Special No. 6: The Vikings* (Crowood, 1999)

Oakeshott, Ewart, *The Sword in the Age of Chivalry* (Boydell & Brewer, 1998)

Oakeshott, Ewart, *Records of the Medieval Sword* (Boydell & Brewer, 1998)

Peirce, Ian, *Swords of the Viking Age*, 5th edition (Boydell & Brewer, 2009)

Pfaff, Peter, *Die Welt der Schweizer Bildchroniken* (Edition 91, 1991)

Richter, Holger, *Die Hornbogenarmbrust. Geschichte und Technik* (Hörnig, 2006)

Spencer, Brian, *Pilgrim Souvenirs and Secular Badges*, 2nd edition (Boydell & Brewer, 2010)

Steuer, Heiko, 'Historische Phasen der Bewaffnung nach Aussagen der archäologischen Quellen Mittel- und Nordeuropas im ersten Jahrtausend n. Chr. In', *Frühmittelalterliche Studien 4* (Gruyter, 1970)

Talhoffer, Hans, *Fechtbuch. Gerichtliche und andere Zweikämpfe darstellend* [1467], 5th edition (VS-BOOKS, 2011)

Thursfield, Sarah, *The Medieval Tailor's Assistant*, 2nd edition (Crowood, 2012)

Thordeman, Bengt, *Armor from the Battle of Wisby 1361* [1939] (Chivalry Bookshelf, 2001)

Tweddle, Dominic, *The Anglian Helmet from Coppergate* (Council for British Archeology, 1992)

Wamers, Egon and Brandt, Michael (eds), *Die Macht des Silbers. Karolingische Schätze im Norden* (Schnell & Steiner, 2005)

Westphal, Herbert, *Franken oder Sachsen? Untersuchungen an frühmittelalterlichen Waffen* (Studien zur Sachsenforschung 14) (Isensee, 2002)

Willemsen, Annemarieke and Ernst, Marlieke, *Hundreds of.... Medieval Chic in Metal. Decorative mounts on belts and purses from the Low Countries, 1300–1600* (Spa, 2012)